TREASURE

THAT LASTS

D0166909

TREASURE

THAT LASTS

TRADING PRIVILEGE, PLEASURE, AND POWER
FOR WHAT REALLY MATTERS

MICHAEL
YOUSSEF

BakerBooks

a division of Baker Publishing Group
Grand Rapids, Michigan

© 2020 by Leacheal, Inc.

Published by Baker Books
a division of Baker Publishing Group
PO Box 6287, Grand Rapids, MI 49516-6287
www.bakerbooks.com

Printed in the United States of America

Library of Congress Cataloging-in-Publication Data
Names: Youssef, Michael, author.
Title: Treasure that lasts : trading privilege, pleasure, and power for what really matters / Michael Youssef.
Description: Grand Rapids, Michigan : Baker Books, a division of Baker Publishing Group, 2020.
Identifiers: LCCN 2020005037 | ISBN 9780801077883 (paperback)
Subjects: LCSH: Moses (Biblical leader) | Decision making—Religious aspects—Christianity. | Choice (Psychology)—Religious aspects—Christianity. | Bible. Exodus—Criticism, interpretation, etc. | Bible. Numbers—Criticism, interpretation, etc.
Classification: LCC BS580.M6 Y685 2020 | DDC 222/.12092—dc23
LC record available at https://lccn.loc.gov/2020005037

ISBN 978-1-5409-0114-9 (hardcover)

Unless otherwise indicated, Scripture quotations are from the Holy Bible, New International Version®. NIV®. Copyright © 1973, 1978, 1984, 2011 by Biblica, Inc.™ Used by permission of Zondervan. All rights reserved worldwide. www.zondervan .com. The "NIV" and "New International Version" are trademarks registered in the United States Patent and Trademark Office by Biblica, Inc.™

Scripture quotations labeled ESV are from are from The Holy Bible, English Standard Version® (ESV®), copyright © 2001 by Crossway, a publishing ministry of Good News Publishers. Used by permission. All rights reserved. ESV Text Edition: 2016

Scriptures quotations labeled KJV are from the King James Version of the Bible.

Some names and identifying details have been changed to protect the privacy of individuals.

20 21 22 23 24 25 26   7 6 5 4 3 2 1

With deep gratitude to the Lord for

Dave and Sally Hangsleben,

a very special couple who have proven
and are continuously pursuing the title of this book—
treasure that lasts.

Contents

Contents

Introduction

The Choice before Us

You have probably never heard of Baron Justinian von Weltz, a Dutch nobleman of the seventeenth century. He had a passion for the gospel of Jesus Christ. Though his story is rarely told today, his zeal for spreading the gospel influenced generations of pastors, teachers, and missionaries.

The first-century church sent out thousands of missionaries from Judea to Europe, Africa, and Asia. But by the seventeenth century, the church had become stagnant. Baron von Weltz, a Lutheran layman, was heartbroken that he and his fellow Lutherans were doing nothing to reach the lost. Like most European nations, Holland had established colonies in Africa, Asia, and the Americas. Yet the Dutch Lutheran church made no effort to reach those lands with the gospel.

Baron von Weltz wrote pamphlets and preached about the need to evangelize the world—but church leaders responded with mockery. He proposed a missionary society

11

called "The Jesus Society" for world evangelism. Eminent Lutheran scholar Johannes Heinrich Ursinus scoffed at the idea, saying that by taking the gospel into godless lands, the Society would draw children of the devil to the church. That, of course, was von Weltz's goal—to draw children of the devil to the gospel and convert them to children of God as Jesus commanded.

In 1664, von Weltz journeyed to Regensburg, Bavaria, to address the Imperial Diet (the ruling council) of the Holy Roman Empire. Once again, he was mocked, as he put it, with "haughty condescension." He added, "I thought the heathen were in far distant lands, and lo, I found myself in the midst of them."

After failing to persuade church leaders to take up the cause of evangelism, von Weltz renounced his title as a baron. With the support of a few close friends, he committed himself to becoming a missionary. In his final sermon before leaving on his missionary journey, he said:

> What is it to me to bear the title "well-born," when I am born again to Christ? What is it to me to have the title "lord," when I desire to be servant of Christ? What is it to me to be called "your grace" when I have need of God's grace? All these vanities I will away with and all else I lay at the feet of my dear Lord Jesus.[1]

Justinian von Weltz set sail for Surinam, a Dutch colony in South America. He arrived in 1666 and died there in 1668. There is no account of von Weltz making a single convert. He lived a lonely life and was buried in a forgotten grave.

Did von Weltz die a failure? Not at all. No one who lives faithfully for God is ever a failure. Though forgotten by the world, Justinian von Weltz was crowned by God with success. God raised up a new generation of believers who read his writings and were inspired to take the gospel to distant corners of the earth. Even in death, his influence ignited a missionary movement that continued expanding long after his death.

Missionary leader Arthur Tappan Pierson said that von Weltz recognized that evangelism is "a Christian duty not to be set aside. For this conviction he surrendered everything—rank, honor, wealth, all the conveniences of life, and, finally, life itself. In his faithfulness to his convictions, he remains a shining example for all times."[2]

Every day, and throughout our lives, we are offered the choice: the world's gold—or God's glory? Justinian von Weltz gave up the world's gold for God's glory. Are you and I willing to do the same?

You've seen the commercials countless times: "Buy gold!" "Invest in gold!" It's no sin to invest for the future. But it is a deadly mistake to choose the world's gold over God's glory.

When I refer to gold, I don't necessarily mean that dense yellow metal whose element symbol is Au and whose atomic number is 79. Our "gold" is anything we treasure, anything that competes with our affection for Jesus Christ. Whatever you value more than God is your "gold." To invest in things that eternally matter, you must turn your back on your "gold," as Justinian von Weltz did—and as Moses did. The Bible tells us, "He [Moses] regarded disgrace for the sake of Christ as of greater value than the treasures of Egypt, because he was looking ahead to his reward" (Heb. 11:26).

By faith, Moses turned his back on the gold of a privileged life in Egypt as the adopted son of Pharaoh. By faith, he chose to become a symbolic Old Testament type of Christ and to be the deliverer of his people. In the coming chapters, we will explore the life of Moses and discover what it means to exchange the world's gold for God's glory. Baron von Weltz chose God's glory over gold—and he began the modern missionary movement. Moses chose God's glory over gold—and he delivered a nation.

As I write these words, the world is in the grip of a global pandemic and a worldwide economic crisis. This crisis did not catch God by surprise. He is using this trial to get the attention of every human being in the world, including the people of his church. Are we listening? Are we turning our hearts toward God? Are we choosing his glory over the gold of this dying world?

In these times that try our souls, we must say to him, "Lord, send me, use me, give me your words to speak. Lord, give me a willing spirit so that I may glorify you in this time of worldwide crisis."

God has set that choice before you and me today—the world's gold or God's glory? What will God accomplish through us if we choose his glory?

Complete Surrender

Overview

Dwight D. Eisenhower was supreme commander of the Allied forces in Europe during World War II and president of the United States from 1953 to 1961. As a young cadet at the United States Military Academy at West Point, he faced a difficult decision: Would he live by the world's values or stay true to his Christian values?

During the fall of 1912 at the beginning of his third year at West Point, Eisenhower was expected to participate in the tradition called "Beast Barracks." During the first six weeks, freshman cadets (called "plebes") were "crawled" (hazed) to reshape them from civilians to cadets. Upperclassmen were expected to make life miserable for the plebes.

One day, Eisenhower saw a plebe running down the hall, so he shouted, "Mr. Dumgard!"—the insulting name applied to all lowly plebes.

The young cadet stopped and stood at attention.

Eisenhower asked what the plebe's PCS ("previous condition of servitude") was, then he added, "You look like a barber."

In a low voice, the plebe said, "I was a barber, sir."

Feeling sick, Eisenhower told the plebe to go on about his business. He went to his barracks and told his roommate, "I'm never going to crawl another plebe as long as I live. . . . I've just done something that was stupid and unforgivable. I managed to make a man ashamed of the work he did to earn a living."[1]

Eisenhower never hazed another incoming cadet. He realized that making young cadets feel ashamed violated his Christian values. He made a decision to forsake the "gold" of West Point tradition in order to glorify God with his life.

The Decisions of Moses

Decision is an interesting word. It comes from a Latin word that literally means "to cut off." That Latin word also gives us the English words *incision* (a surgical cut) and *scissors* (a cutting implement). When we make a decision, we cut off all other courses of action.

The story of Moses is the story of a man who made decisions—a man who chose one course of action and cut off all other options and possibilities. In Acts 7, Stephen, the first Christian martyr, stood before the Sanhedrin—the same ruling council that had condemned Jesus to death—and recounted the story of Moses. He divided the life of Moses into three segments of forty years. Each of those forty-year points was marked by a major decision.

Moses spent the first forty years in the palace of the Pharaoh, learning that he was something and somebody. He spent the second forty years in the desert, learning that he was nothing and nobody. He spent the final forty years leading the Israelites out of Egypt and through the desert, learning that God is everything.

Moses could have remained in the palace, living in the lap of luxury. But, as Stephen told the Sanhedrin, Moses had a decision to make: cling to the gold and treasures of Egypt, or identify with God's people. Stephen said, "When Moses was forty years old, he decided to visit his own people, the Israelites" (v. 23).

This decision set in motion a chain of events that would shape the course of his life. Moses saw an Egyptian beating an Israelite, so he stepped in and killed the Egyptian. He thought the Israelites would be grateful he had taken their side—but the Israelites accused him of murdering the Egyptian. So Moses fled and hid in the desert.

Had Moses not made that crucial decision to visit his people, had he chosen to remain in the palace, we would never have read his story in the Bible. Instead, we would have read about him in the secular history books about ancient Egypt. His whole life would barely have rated a single paragraph—the only Hebrew slave to become a Pharaoh. The entire history of Israel might never have happened if Moses had not made that fateful decision. Because of that

decision, he killed an Egyptian, then fled into the wilderness.
Forty years after that first decision, God confronted Moses
with another life-altering decision:

> After forty years had passed, an angel appeared to Moses
> in the flames of a burning bush in the desert near Mount
> Sinai. When he saw this, he was amazed at the sight. As
> he went over to get a closer look, he heard the Lord say: "I
> am the God of your fathers, the God of Abraham, Isaac
> and Jacob." Moses trembled with fear and did not dare to
> look.
>
> Then the Lord said to him, "Take off your sandals, for the
> place where you are standing is holy ground. I have indeed
> seen the oppression of my people in Egypt. I have heard their
> groaning and have come down to set them free. Now come,
> I will send you back to Egypt." (vv. 30–34)

Moses decided to spend the rest of his life seeking not gold
but the glory of God. He was fearful, he was reluctant, yet
he made a decision that cut off all other options. He decided
to follow the Lord.

The Man Who Had Everything

Moses was a man on a mission. He obeyed God's commands
at great personal risk. How many people today would willingly give up wealth and power for a life of hardship and
servanthood? Fame and position produce honor. Powerful
political families often set themselves up as dynasties, trading
on their fame, acquiring wealth and power that often lead
to greed, corruption, and the abuse of power. That's why

God values and approves of those who choose his glory over the world's gold.

God presented Moses with a choice, and Moses chose obedience. Every one of us has been invited and called by God. We have a choice to obey him or rebel against him, to receive him or reject him, to choose his glory or the world's gold. Disobedience may offer short-term gratification, but it always leads to destruction. Solomon wrote:

> There is a way that appears to be right,
> but in the end it leads to death. (Prov. 14:12)

You've heard about "the man who has everything," and that describes Moses. People waited on Moses hand and foot. He could spend every morning on the golf course and every afternoon in the palace Jacuzzi. He could order the best foods, wear the best clothes, and enjoy the best recreational pastimes. Luxuries are not sinful per se, but those luxuries would have been sin for Moses because God had called him out of the palace and into the adventure of faith.

God's Word commends Moses because he gave up the world's gold for God's glory. He gave up everything that stood in the way of perfect obedience. Is God calling you from the burning bush? What is the choice he has set before you? Have you made the decision to cut off all other options to pursue God's will for your life? What is the gold that has you in its grip, keeping you from abandoning yourself to God's will and his glory?

We've read Stephen's biography of Moses. Now let's look at another New Testament commentary on the life of Moses, this time from Hebrews: "He [Moses] regarded disgrace for the sake of Christ as of greater value than the treasures of Egypt, because he was looking ahead to his reward" (Heb. 11:26).

Moses considered what it would mean to follow God's will. He thought carefully about what it would cost him to accept God's calling. He weighed the pros and the cons. He did a cost-benefit analysis. He knew that he would bring disgrace on himself if he identified with the Israelite slaves— yet he considered that disgrace to be of greater value than all the treasures of the kingdom of Egypt. In the end, Moses decided that the worst this world could do to him would bring him a far greater reward than the best this world could offer him.

It's fascinating that the writer to the Hebrews phrases it this way: "He regarded disgrace for the sake of Christ . . ." How could this be? Moses had never heard of Jesus Christ. In fact, Moses lived more than fifteen hundred years before Christ was born. How, then, could Moses make a decision "for the sake of Christ"?

Every believer who was saved in Old Testament times was saved on the same basis that you and I are saved as Christians: we are all saved by the blood of Jesus the Messiah. In Old Testament times, believers were saved by faith as they looked forward to the coming of the Messiah. In New Testament times and up to the present day, believers are saved by faith as they look backward to the cross.

Moses was saved by grace through faith in Jesus—fifteen hundred years before Jesus was born. Does that mean that Moses lived a perfect life? In the chapters to come, we'll see Moses stumble and fall. We'll see him try to accomplish God's will in his own strength—and he will fail miserably.

He will try to take God's purposes into his own hands—and he'll make a complete mess of things. God will have to tear Moses down, then build him up again before Moses can be a true instrument of God.

Yet through it all, Moses stood firm on his decision to give up the world's gold for God's glory. That decision, made in the presence of God at the burning bush, will sustain him, keep him focused, and empower him so that God can use him in a mighty way as Israel's deliverer and lawgiver.

I once heard someone say, "If it's a contest between Egypt and Moses, pity Moses. But if it's a contest between Egypt and God, pity Egypt." God promises that the moment you turn your back on this world's gold in order to pursue God's glory, he will accomplish great things through you. Trading gold for glory produces incalculable rewards.

By Faith . . .

Exodus 12:40 tells us that from the time Joseph entered Egypt until Moses led the Israelites out of Egypt was a span of 430 years. In Genesis 15:13–14, God told Abraham that his descendants would be enslaved in a foreign land for four centuries, after which God would rescue them. Just as God had said, Abraham's great-grandson, Joseph, was sold into slavery in Egypt by his envious brothers, but Joseph rose to power and brought his family to Egypt, where they became very numerous. A new Pharaoh looked at all the Israelites in his borders and saw them as a threat, feeling their numbers would overwhelm the Egyptian population. So Pharaoh

21

oppressed the Israelites, forcing them to make bricks for Egypt's many construction projects.

But at the right moment in history, God raised up Moses to deliver the Israelites from slavery in Egypt. God had prepared Moses for this role—first by raising him in Pharaoh's household for forty years, then by refining him in the wilderness for another forty years. In the palace, Moses learned the inner workings of leadership and the Egyptian government. In the wilderness, he learned character, faith, endurance, perseverance, and humility.

Moses had everything he could have wanted in Pharaoh's palace, yet he surrendered it all to become Israel's deliverer. Does Moses remind you of anyone? Does this description of Moses resonate in your mind? Does Moses seem to be a type or symbol of someone else in the Bible—someone you are well acquainted with? Of course, he does.

Jesus, the Son of God, gave up every privilege and benefit of being one with the Father in heaven. He came to earth as humanity's deliverer. He gave up the riches of heaven for the sake of God's glory. Moses foreshadowed the coming of Jesus the Messiah.

Hebrews 11 is known as the "Hall of Faith." It's a list of great Old Testament role models of faith—Abel, Enoch, Noah, Abraham, Isaac, Jacob, Joseph, Moses, and on and on. Again and again, the writer of the book of Hebrews tells us, "By faith Abel brought God a better offering; by faith Noah . . . built an ark; by faith . . . Abraham obeyed and went" (vv. 4, 7, 8). All the heroes listed in Hebrews 11 have one thing in common: faith.

Throughout the Bible, the word *faith* is interchangeable with the word *obedience*. You cannot have one without the other. Faith requires obedience and obedience requires faith.

Read through the four Gospels, and you will never see Jesus commending his disciples for their intelligence, their wisdom, their zeal, or their strategic thinking. What does he continually, pointedly talk about? Faith. Faith like a mustard seed can uproot a sycamore tree or cast a mountain into the sea. Faith casts out demons. Faith manifests the power of God in the darkest circumstances.

We hear a lot about faith these days—but much of what preachers (especially TV preachers) say about faith is unbiblical nonsense. They tell you that you should have faith to be wealthy, faith to be healthy, faith to "name it and claim it," faith to drive a Cadillac and own a private jet and live in a hilltop mansion.

The kind of faith these preachers sell is not what the Bible calls faith. It's not obedience. It's what is called (in secular circles) "the power of positive thinking." It's a worldly and self-centered kind of faith. It's the false faith of what is known as the prosperity gospel. Moses was a man of faith—but not the faith of the prosperity gospel. He already possessed more prosperity than you and I could imagine—but he turned his back on it all to pursue God's glory.

According to the Word of God, faith is the willingness to let God rule supreme in every situation. Authentic faith says, "Have thine own way, Lord." Authentic faith agrees with John the Baptist, who said, "He must increase, but I must decrease" (John 3:30 KJV).

By faith, Moses renounced his wealth and position. By faith, he renounced power and prestige. By faith, he identified with God's persecuted people, not the ruling class. Pharaoh saw the faith of Moses as folly. The faith of Moses makes no sense in this selfish, greedy, me-first world. The faith of Moses defies the logic of the secular mind.

Moses didn't have to go out among his people. He could have easily rationalized sitting comfortably in the palace of Pharaoh. He could have told himself, *I can do more for my people from inside the palace than as an outsider*. God does call some Christians to work within the government, the media, academia, or the business world in order to be a witness and an agent of change in those institutions. But for Moses, that would have been disobedience. God called him out of the palace and to a place of godly leadership of the Israelite nation.

By faith, Moses gave up the world's gold for God's glory. Does this mean God calls every Christian to a life of hardship and poverty? No, he does not. What God asks of you may not be what he asks of me or of someone else. But each of us has some form of gold in our lives, and that gold tempts us to settle for less than God's glory in our lives.

"It's Complete Surrender"

If you have seen the 1981 motion picture *Chariots of Fire*, you know something of the life of Eric Liddell—but you may not know the whole story. Born to a Scottish missionary couple in northern China in 1902, he was educated at a boarding school in south London. He emerged as the fastest runner in Scotland, and his reputation as an athlete gave him

Peut de chval!

a platform for sharing his Christian testimony at student evangelistic meetings.

In 1923, he set the United Kingdom's record for the 100-yard dash at 9.7 seconds. He was set to compete at the 1924 Paris Olympics, but when the heat for the 100-yard race was scheduled for Sunday, he refused to run. Though it was an agonizing decision, Eric viewed Sunday as the Lord's Day, the Christian Sabbath, a day of rest. He believed his Christian testimony would suffer and that it would be a sin if he ran on the Lord's Day.

Many sports writers and fans criticized Eric Liddell's decision, and some accused him of being unpatriotic. Even the Prince of Wales tried to change his mind. Liddell refused to bow to pressure and compromise his convictions.

Liddell trained for the 400-yard race, even though he was not considered as strong a runner at that distance. On the morning of the Olympic final, Eric's masseur handed him a handwritten note that read, "In the old book it says, 'He that honours me I will honour.' Wishing you the best of success always."[2]

Inspired by this message, Liddell won the race, set a world record of 47.6 seconds, and won the gold medal. Though he could have gained fame and fortune as a professional athlete, he chose to give up the world's gold—the 100-yard-dash gold medal—for God's glory.

Preaching at an evangelistic rally in Scotland, Eric Liddell summed up his view of life this way: "Many of us are missing something in life because we are after the second-best. . . . We are putting before you the one who is worthy of all of our devotion—Christ. He is the Savior . . . and He is the one who can bring out the best that is in us."[3]

Liddell went on to devote himself to missionary work in China. There he served the poor and preached the good news of Jesus Christ. In 1943, the Imperial Japanese Army overran the mission station where he served. He and other members of the China Inland Mission were imprisoned. Liddell emerged as a leader who encouraged the morale and faith of his fellow prisoners. Despite the starvation rations, filth, and disease of the prison, Liddell demonstrated kindness, good will, and cheerfulness to everyone.

He became sick, and at first it seemed that his illness was merely the result of overwork and malnutrition. He died on February 21, 1945, five months before the prison was liberated. After his death, an autopsy revealed he had died of a brain tumor, and his death was undoubtedly hastened by the harsh conditions in the prison.

His last words were "It's complete surrender."[4] That's how Eric Liddell lived and died—surrendering the world's gold while pursuing God's glory.

What are you living for? Are you living a life of complete surrender?

■ QUESTIONS FOR REFLECTION AND DISCUSSION ■

1. In your understanding of the Bible, how do you define *faith*?
2. Do you sense that God is leading you to a specific calling or mission? Who or what was the "burning bush" God used to get your attention?

3. Have you reached the point in your Christian walk where you view disgrace for the sake of Christ as more valuable than gold? Why or why not?

4. Eric Liddell's last words were "It's complete surrender." On a scale of 1 to 10, with 1 being completely self-willed and 10 being completely surrendered, how surrendered are you? What is the gold that has you in its grip?

God, bring. out. The best in. you. That's what's

importantl Stay Home, Maybe Consider. Gas

By Mileage an

Yes, Cars.

Heir to Power—and Poverty

Exodus 1:1–2:10

My mother was just past the middle of the second trimester of pregnancy. Her health was precarious, and her doctors told her there was a good chance she would not survive giving birth to me. They urged her to have a therapeutic abortion to save her life, and the abortion procedure was scheduled.

The night before the abortion was to take place, the pastor of our church came and told my parents, "Do not have the abortion. Trust God. He has his hand on your life and the life of your unborn baby. The child you are carrying shall be born to serve the Lord."

My parents accepted the pastor's word as a message from God. They refused the abortion, and four months later, my mother gave birth to me. She survived childbirth and lived to see me surrender my life to the Lord when I was sixteen.

God has a special place in his heart for children—and so should we. Our children are under attack by the god of this world, Satan. When I see some of the blatant schemes being carried out by our government and our educational establishment—schemes to destroy the family and erode respect for marriage and the protection of children—I can easily become discouraged.

Thankfully, God doesn't let my discouragement last long. He sends the Holy Spirit to remind me of all the ways he has had a hand on my life. When I should have been aborted, God had the last word. When I grew up in a Muslim land, surrounded by people and institutions hostile to the Christian faith, God had the last word. Again and again, when the odds were against me, God was for me, and he had the last word.

Today our government bans prayer and God's Word from schools while aggressively teaching godlessness and immorality to our children. Though we need to do all we can to protect our children from the corrosive influence of government-controlled education and indoctrination, we should also remember that our God is greater than the schemes of the devil and the plans of atheists, communists, Islamists, radicals, and government officials. The greater the hostility, the mightier our children will be as we arm them for the spiritual battles ahead.

Born under a Death Sentence

If you look at the lives of great men and women in God's Word, you find they all had people in their lives who taught

29

them, inspired them, affirmed them, and invested in them. Someone exercised faith on their behalf. Someone prayed for them. Someone trained them in the way they should go.

From his early childhood, the prophet Samuel was mentored and trained by Eli, the priest of Shiloh. The greatness of David, the shepherd king, can be traced to the influence and prayers of the prophet Samuel.

In the New Testament, Jesus taught, trained, and prayed for the Twelve, eleven of whom would become the foundation of the church. When the apostle Paul was a young man, he studied the Jewish law under the scholar Gamaliel and later learned about the grace of Jesus Christ from Ananias of Damascus and Barnabas the Encourager. Paul mentored young Timothy, who pastored the church in Ephesus, but Timothy's earliest spiritual influences were his mother, Eunice, and grandmother Lois.

History tells us that Augustine was deeply influenced for God by his praying mother, Monica. And John and Charles Wesley were trained for the ministry by their praying mother, Susanna. The list goes on and on. Children and young adults need people in their corner who will pray, be role models, and invest in their lives.

Though Moses was a man who gave up the world's gold for God's glory, he didn't grow up in a vacuum. There were influences in his life that shaped him and prepared him for the role God had chosen him to play.

Moses was born under a death sentence. Exodus 1 tells us that the descendants of Joseph and his brothers grew so numerous in Egypt "that the land was filled with them" (Exod. 1:7). Joseph, the great-grandson of Abraham, had brought his father, Israel, and his siblings to Egypt, a total of about seventy Israelite family members. Over four centuries, those seventy Israelites became two million Israelites, a nation within a nation.

Then a new Pharaoh arose "to whom Joseph meant nothing" (v. 8). Because the Israelite slaves were so numerous, Pharaoh feared that in a time of war, the Israelites might side with the enemy and fight against the Egyptians. He didn't care that Joseph, the Hebrew forefather, had saved Egypt from starvation. That was ancient history. This new Pharaoh felt threatened by the Israelites. He wanted to abolish the old policy of welcoming the Israelites as equals. Though he felt threatened by the Israelites, he couldn't live without them because they were a source of cheap labor.

So Pharaoh devised a diabolical three-pronged plan to control the growth of the Hebrew nation. First prong: demoralize the Israelites. Second prong: decrease their number. Third prong: destroy their future.

He wanted, first, to wear the Israelites down physically, emotionally, and spiritually. Pharaoh ordered the Egyptian slave masters to oppress the Israelites. He wanted to demoralize them by working them to a state of exhaustion while terrorizing them with fear of punishment.

He wanted, second, to prevent them from having male children—for without male children, the Hebrew nation would be unable to reproduce. This would decrease their number. Such a plan comes straight from the mind of Satan. Down through history, Satan has moved various nations to try to wipe Israel from the face of the earth. Anti-Semitism and genocide are Satan's go-to plots against God's chosen people from Bible times right up to the present day.

Inspired by Satan, Pharaoh ordered the Hebrew midwives to murder the male Israelite babies as soon as they were born. The Hebrew midwives disobeyed Pharaoh and let the Israelite babies live. At great personal risk, the midwives told Pharaoh that the Hebrew women were so vigorous that they gave birth before the midwives could arrive. They risked their lives to save the lives of the Hebrew baby boys.

I believe a time is coming when our own children will have to risk their lives to remain faithful to God's Word. That's why we need to train them today, so that they will courageously, faithfully stand up and be counted when the time of testing comes.

The second prong of Pharaoh's plan had failed, so he went to the third prong: destroy the future of the Israelites. To do this, he ordered the Egyptians to drown all the Hebrew boys in the Nile. It was during the time of this death sentence against Hebrew boys that Moses was born to a Levite couple (Exod. 2). Moses's parents already had two children before this edict was issued, Moses's brother, Aaron, and sister, Miriam.

Pharaoh was an idolater who worshiped the Egyptian crocodile god. By ordering the Hebrew babies to be thrown into the Nile, he was getting rid of God's people while making human sacrifices to his god, the crocodiles of the Nile.

Many people today—including many who call themselves "Christians"—claim that Satan does not exist. But look at the long march of history:

- the genocidal plot of Pharaoh against the Jews in Exodus
- the Assyrian and Babylonian massacres and exiles of the Jews from their homeland

- Haman's plot against the Jews in Persia in the time of Queen Esther
- the countless pogroms and massacres of Jews in Europe in the Middle Ages
- the pogroms across Russia in the eighteenth through twentieth centuries
- the Nazi Holocaust during World War II
- the attacks against the modern state of Israel by Muslim nations
- the attacks against Jews by Al Qaida, ISIS, and other terrorist groups

How else do you explain the consistent, concerted effort by many different nations and cultures, in many eras of history, against one people—the Jews, God's chosen people, the people out of whom the Messiah was born? There must be one diabolical mind behind all these disparate attempts to destroy the Jewish people.

The centuries-long campaign against the Jews begins here, in Egypt, as wailing Hebrew mothers have their baby boys snatched from their breasts and flung into the Nile. Into this age of terror and sorrow, Moses was born.

Heir to Egyptian Power and Israelite Poverty

Because of Pharaoh's death sentence against Hebrew boys, Moses's mother, Jochebed, hid baby Moses for three months. When she realized she couldn't keep him hidden much longer, she used tar to waterproof a papyrus basket. Then she placed baby Moses in the basket and set it adrift among the reeds along the Nile riverbank. When Pharaoh's daughter went to the river to bathe, she found the basket with baby Moses, and she adopted the baby as her own. Moses's sister, Miriam, arranged for Pharaoh's daughter to hire Jochebed to nurse the baby.

Years later, Moses learned the story of his birth. He knew he was born an Israelite under Pharaoh's death sentence. Though Moses was raised in the household of the Egyptian Pharaoh, Exodus 2 makes it clear that he identified with his people, the Israelites.

Moses was born and raised under unique conditions. He was the son of Israelite slaves yet raised in the palace of the Egyptian king. He was saved from death by an Egyptian princess yet nursed by his enslaved Israelite mother. With one foot in the world of Egyptian royalty and the other in the slave camps of Israel, Moses was uniquely qualified for the task God had planned for him. He understood the world of Egyptian power and wealth, and he understood the world of Israelite powerlessness and poverty.

Ultimately, it was the faith and commitment of his parents under God's sovereign plan that made Moses a champion for God. Moses's mother trusted God and prayed for baby Moses as she set him alone on the waters of the Nile. Her decision to place that baby in a tar-lined basket among the reeds seems like a small matter in the grand scheme of things—yet that decision was the hinge of history that God used to move the Hebrew people from slavery to liberty, from extinction to nationhood, from death in Egypt to life in the promised land.

Thank God that Moses's mother, Jochebed, and father, Amram, lived out their courageous faith instead of obeying their fears. Because of their faith, Moses lived to become the deliverer and lawgiver of Israel. Godly courage prays in faith; godly courage plans in hope; godly courage teaches in confidence; godly courage entrusts the outcome to God. The courage of the godly is expressed in the words of the psalmist:

> Whoever dwells in the shelter of the Most High
> will rest in the shadow of the Almighty.
> I will say of the LORD, "He is my refuge and my
> fortress,
> my God, in whom I trust." (Ps. 91:1–2)

Moses's parents, Jochebed and Amram, came from the tribe of Levi, and they were faithful to God in the midst of a faithless society. Not only did they live in the hostile, pagan society of Egypt but also the majority of their Hebrew friends and relatives had given themselves over to Egyptian idolatry. The Israelites were so steeped in pagan practices that fifty years after they left Egypt, Joshua said to them: "Now fear the LORD and serve him with all faithfulness. Throw away the gods your ancestors worshiped beyond the Euphrates River and in Egypt, and serve the LORD" (Josh. 24:14). Even after all the miraculous signs God performed on their behalf, the Israelites remained mired in the sinful practices of Egypt.

Moses's family faced opposition on every side. They were part of a very small remnant of faithful people. They trusted God's promise to Abraham, and they kept the faith of Abraham, Isaac, and Jacob.

There are important parallels between the world of Moses's day and the twenty-first-century world in which we live.

Even when the whole world has gone mad, God still honors the faith of faithful parents. Even when the faith community has abandoned the truth, God will honor those who hold fast to his Word.

Hebrews 11:23 tells us, "By faith Moses' parents hid him for three months after he was born, because they saw he was no ordinary child, and they were not afraid of the king's edict." Jochebed and Amram trusted God to preserve the life of their child from Pharaoh.

Can you imagine the fear and torment those parents must have felt during the three months they kept Moses hidden from the Egyptian government? Any time he cried, an Egyptian soldier or spy might hear—and baby Moses could lose his life. Any knock on the door might mean a visit from their baby's executioner. Any neighbor who asked a question—even a Hebrew neighbor—might be an informant for the government. Their emotions must have swung wildly from faith to fear and back again.

Faith conquers fear every time—but faith must be renewed by continual prayer and meditation on God's truth. As Jochebed renewed her faith in God, she gained the courage to follow God's plan. She placed the baby in a basket and set it afloat on the very waters that Pharaoh had decreed to be the instrument of the baby's death.

A Sense of Ironic Justice

The Nile was the source of life in Egypt, but Pharaoh had turned it into a source of sorrow and grief. God, in his mercy, restored the Nile's life-giving function in the life of Moses

36

and his family. When you are in God's protective program, even the enemy's instrument of death becomes a source of life.

I've often said, "I am invincible—until God says it's time for me to come home." I believe that with all my heart. No disease or enemy or accident can take my life until God decides my life has been completed.

I wonder if Moses's parents studied the ebb and the flow of the Nile. I wonder if they knew exactly when and where Pharaoh's daughter regularly came to bathe in the Nile. Perhaps the Egyptian princess was miraculously drawn there by the hand of God alone—but then again, perhaps Moses's parents diligently planned and worked out a timetable of events even as they prayed for God's provision and protection. We don't know and it ultimately doesn't matter.

What does matter is that, by faith, Moses's parents placed the basket at the right place at the right time. Meanwhile, Moses's big sister, Miriam, hid in the bushes, watching and waiting. As soon as Pharaoh's daughter found the baby in the basket, Miriam popped up and said, "You need a nurse for that baby? Have I got a nurse for you!"

Pharaoh's daughter knew that the baby in the basket was a Hebrew baby. She may have wondered at the coincidence of a Hebrew girl showing up at just the right time—or she may have suspected that Miriam knew more about that baby than she let on. In any case, the Egyptian princess was glad to have help caring for the foundling.

There are ironies in this account that can only be appreciated through the eyes of faith. First, Jochebed got to save her baby's life and nurse her own baby, and she even got paid to do so. Second, Jochebed got to nurse her baby under the protection of Pharaoh's guards—the very guards who had been commanded to kill the Hebrew babies. Third, it was Pharaoh's own daughter, the princess of Egypt, who disobeyed his command—a disobedience that led to the liberation of the Israelites and the destruction of the Egyptian army in the Red Sea.

I think God must have been amused to not only thwart the plans of Pharaoh and the plans of Satan but to do so with a sense of ironic justice. We would miss out on these facets of the story of Moses if we read it from the perspective of an unbeliever, a cynic, an agnostic, or an atheist. Only when you view the story through the lens of faith do all the meaningful details come into focus.

If you are a parent or a grandparent, I urge you to apply the lessons of Moses's early life to your own family. Let me suggest three practical lessons from this ancient story that still speak to us, forcefully and profoundly, in the twenty-first century.

First, implement God's plan for your children. God has his hand on the lives of your children and grandchildren. Teach them, train them, pray for them, encourage them, build their character and courage and faith so that they can withstand the testing of the coming days.

Second, practice your faith openly and unashamedly in front of them. Let them see you praying, reading your Bible, applying your faith to everyday situations, and sharing your faith with the people around you. Set a good example of active, living Christianity so that they will follow your example as they grow up. It's important to teach your children God's truth, but they learn so much more about what it means to be a Christian when they catch you in the act of being a courageous, faithful believer.

Third, unite with other believers in your walk of faith. You are much more likely to take a courageous stand for Christ when you don't have to stand alone. The name *Moses* means "snatched out," and every believer in Christ has been "snatched out" from among those who are perishing. We have been snatched out of the clutches of Satan and the jaws of hell.

Why did God save us from sin and condemnation? Why did he draw us up out of the river of death? So that we may glorify the name of Jesus. Life is not about amassing the gold of this world for ourselves. It's about giving God the glory he is due.

▦ QUESTIONS FOR REFLECTION AND DISCUSSION ▦

1. Down through history, no single ethnic group has been so viciously targeted for destruction as the Jewish people. How does the preservation of God's chosen people impact your faith?

2. Moses was born under a death sentence in a hostile land. Today, your children and grandchildren live in a world that is hostile to Christianity. What steps can you take to safeguard their faith?

3. Many Israelites adopted the idolatrous religion of Egypt. But the family of Moses remained faithful to the God of Abraham, Isaac, and Jacob. Do you find

it easy or difficult to maintain your faith and your Christian witness today?

4. Moses was raised with one foot in the royal house of Egypt and the other in the slave camps of the Israelites. His upbringing uniquely qualified him for the task God had planned for him. How has God uniquely prepared you to serve him? Are you playing the role he prepared for you?

5. Moses's mother taught him to love God. Who are the children that you are influencing for God today? Do they see you reading your Bible and telling others about Jesus? Why or why not?

Stepping-Stones
to Leadership

Exodus 2:11–25

Moses's birth mother was privileged to help raise him during his crucial early years. But by the time Moses reached the age of five or six, his birth parents had to relinquish Moses to Pharaoh's daughter, who became Moses's adoptive mother.

Those early years with his mother proved to be vitally important in Moses's development. I'm sure that his birth parents took every opportunity to fill his heart with stories of God's faithfulness to Abraham, to Joseph, and to his people, the Israelites.

The First Five Years Fund (FFYF), an organization devoted to enhancing the lives of children through early learning experiences, reports that over "one million new neural connections are formed every second in the first few years of life." That is why the first five years of life are crucial to the kind of human being the child will become, as an FFYF report explains:

> During the first five years, a child's brain is at its most flexible, making this a critical period for learning and growth. . . . Prolonged stress during childhood can do damage to a child's brain architecture, which can lead to lifelong problems in learning, behavior, and physical and mental health. . . .
>
> Supportive, responsive relationships with caring adults as early in life as possible can prevent or reverse the damaging effects of toxic stress in children.[1]

Those first few years that Moses enjoyed with his birth mother were his most formative years. They were the foundation for the rest of his life. His mother gave him an essential understanding of who he was, who his people were, and who his God was.

After that foundation had been laid, Moses received thirty-five years of the best secular education the Egyptian culture had to offer—but the Egyptians could not erase those crucial early years of godly training.

At that time, the ancient Egyptians had the first known written language. The Egyptians excelled in mathematics and geometry. They had advanced knowledge of astronomy and architecture. Their medical knowledge was the most advanced of that era, and they were the first to develop techniques of brain surgery and dentistry. Their knowledge of the art of war was second to none.

Moses was probably trained at the Temple of Heliopolis, which was the Oxford or Harvard of the ancient world.

The Jewish historian Josephus, in chapter 10 of *Antiquities of the Jews*, Book II, records an account not found in the Bible. In that account, Moses was appointed a general over the Egyptian army. In that leadership role, Josephus wrote, Moses led Egypt to victory in a war against Ethiopia. It is impossible to say whether this account is true or not. But in view of everything we know about Moses from the Scriptures, it is not unlikely that Moses served as a military leader in Egypt.

Right Motives, Wrong Timing

Moses was a physically strong man. Acts 7:22 tells us, "Moses was educated in all the wisdom of the Egyptians and was powerful in speech and action." And in Exodus 2:11–12, we read that Moses "saw an Egyptian beating a Hebrew, one of his own people. Looking this way and that and seeing no one, he killed the Egyptian and hid him in the sand." The Egyptian evidently had no chance to put up a struggle or leave a mark on Moses, which suggests that Moses might have killed the Egyptian with a single blow.

Moses was an adopted member of the Egyptian royal family. When he raced around in his golden chariot, the people bowed before him. When he sailed the Nile on his royal yacht, crowds lined the riverbank to catch a glimpse of him. Moses was a celebrity in Egypt. It would have been easy for his wealth, power, and fame to go to his head.

But Moses had been instructed well in those early, formative years. He remembered all the stories and spiritual principles his Israelite birth mother taught him. He remembered the God of Abraham, Isaac, and Jacob. He remembered his people and their suffering. He undoubtedly wondered how God might use him to deliver them from the slave-master's whip. The day he saw an Egyptian slave driver beating an Israelite, all his righteous indignation came boiling to the surface. He couldn't free all the Israelite people— but he could stop this beating.

Moses thought he was doing the right thing for the right reason. He thought he was following God. He seized the moment and he acted, but he acted in anger. He acted in the heat of the moment. He didn't pray. He didn't seek the mind of God. Instead, he committed murder. Perhaps he thought the man he saved would be grateful and would tell his fellow Israelites that Moses was on their side. Perhaps he thought that by killing the Egyptian, he would spark a slave rebellion leading to liberation for his people.

He had the right motives, but the wrong timing—and he took the wrong action. God did not call Moses to commit murder. God had a different plan, and God was operating on a different timetable.

Notice the details in the Exodus account: "Looking this way and that and seeing no one, he killed the Egyptian" (v. 12). Here's a principle you can be sure of: when you're doing something wrong, when you are contemplating an act of sin, you will look to the right and to the left to see if anyone is watching. But when you know you are doing God's will, when you are seeking to please and glorify the Lord, you don't care who is watching or what they will say. You only want to please God.

44

Not only did Moses kill the Egyptian slave driver, but he also buried the evidence. When you sin, you will try to bury the consequences of your sin. Moses thought, *If I bury this Egyptian in the sand, no one will know*. Does that kind of thinking sound familiar?

Perhaps you are engaged in some activity that you want to keep hidden. You think, *If I cover my tracks well, if I am careful, if I delete the texts from my phone and erase my browser history, if I destroy the receipts and I'm careful which credit card I use, no one will know what I'm doing*. Such thinking is delusional. We are fooling ourselves.

How many headlines have you seen in which some rich and powerful person got away with secret affairs or secret crimes for years—and then it all came tumbling out into the open? As Moses himself said to the people of Israel (speaking from tragic experience), "You may be sure that your sin will find you out" (Num. 32:23).

You can try to bury the result of your disobedience. You can try to bury your secret sin. You can try to hide the evidence—but it will haunt you. It will lurk in your memories and trouble your sleep and interfere with your relationships with people and God. There is only one place where our sins can truly be buried for good, and that place is the cross of Jesus.

Whenever you contemplate an action, and you look this way and that way because you want to be sure there are no witnesses, remember that you are in a danger zone. You are putting yourself in jeopardy. Heed the warning of Moses: your sins will find you out.

God's University of Faith

But didn't Moses act selflessly? Wasn't he defending the oppressed? Wasn't he sincere in his desire to help his people? The answer to all those questions is yes. Moses is proof that you can do what you think is right, you can do it with the best motives, you can do it with the utmost sincerity—and you may still be violating the will and moral law of God.

Whenever we contemplate taking action to right a wrong, we need to ask ourselves: Is this the will of God? Is this what God is commanding me to do? Is this action consistent with the Word of God? Am I acting out of pride and self-will, or am I acting in obedience to God?

You might say, "But if I question every action that way, I'll never do anything. Isn't all of this questioning just a prescription for procrastination?"

The answer is no. It's wise to get into a habit of praying before big decisions, asking God to probe our motives and to reveal any sinful intentions in our hearts. The more we practice a spiritual, godly approach to decision making, the more we will attune our hearts to hear the voice of God. The more attuned we are to God and his leading, the more ready and confident our decision making will be.

There's no substitute for obedience. If we are sincerely seeking to obey God's will, then even when we make mistakes, he will give us another chance. Our God is the Lord of the second chance. And of the third chance. And of the hundredth.

Here, in Exodus 2, Moses failed in his first chance. As a result, he will spend forty years in God's University of

Faith. We will see that Moses was reared in the palace of the pagans, yet he espoused the cause of God's people. He was nursed in the lap of luxury, yet he embraced the desert of adversity. He was educated in the ways of the despot, yet he became a champion of liberty. An heir of the Egyptian oppressor, he took up the cause of the oppressed Israelites. He rejected the crown of Pharaoh and took up the cross of Christ.

But first Moses had to learn that there is a price to be paid when we try to do God's work in our own way. Moses had to spend some time in God's University of Faith, learning that his sin would find him out. Are you studying the same curriculum Moses studied? Are you finding the lessons of God's University of Faith to be hard, and even crushing? Remember, graduation day is coming. God is preparing you to apply the lessons you are learning right now.

Broken to Serve

Imagine you are the son of the Egyptian princess, an heir to the throne of the Pharaoh. You have everything going for you: wealth, fame, power, and status. You have the world at your feet, and you are one of the most admired celebrities of the ancient world. You can do no wrong.

What is wrong with this picture? Answer: God can't use you.

God doesn't use powerful, arrogant, unbroken people as instruments of his will. Even when he used the pagan king of Babylon, Nebuchadnezzar, he had to break him first. So

God had to break Moses in order to use him. God had to tear down Moses's arrogance, self-confidence, and compulsive self-will so that he could build Moses up to become a champion of justice and liberation.

We see this principle in the lives of many other heroes of the faith. God had to break Jacob's strength at Peniel (Gen. 32) to transform self-willed Jacob (whose name means "one who takes the place of another") into a patriarch named Israel ("God contends").

When Gideon blew the trumpet at night (Judg. 7), his three hundred select soldiers broke their earthen pitchers, revealing the light of the torches within, giving them the victory over the terrorized Midianites.

Jesus broke the five loaves of bread (Matt. 14) and used that broken bread to feed five thousand men, women, and children.

Mary, the sister of Martha and Lazarus, had to break her alabaster box of ointment (Mark 14; John 12) to anoint Jesus and fill the room with a beautiful fragrance.

And it was only when Jesus allowed his holy, sinless body to be broken on the cross that redemption was poured out on all repentant sinners.

Yes, God specializes in turning brokenness into beauty and redemption for us—and glory for himself. In your times of brokenness, rejoice—you are about to experience greater blessing than you ever thought possible.

When Moses acted out of emotions and rage, the result was extreme brokenness in his life. But God uses the brokenness we bring on ourselves to produce healing in our lives and glory for himself.

Willing to Be Willing

Acting out of emotion instead of obedience is a spiritual slippery slope. It always leads downward to a worse attitude and more sinful behavior. You will continue that downward spiral of anger, reaction, more anger, bigger reaction, until you finally stop and call out, "Lord, help me! I'm not behaving like a Christian anymore! I'm not even thinking like a follower of Christ anymore! Save me from my out-of-control emotions!"

George H. C. Macgregor was a Scottish preacher who made a major impact for Christ in nineteenth-century England, especially at Keswick and other Christian conferences. He believed that the key to the victorious Christian life is the total consecration of our will to God. He wrote:

> The will is the central faculty of the human soul; it is that which makes us what we are. When the will is given up to God, the citadel of man's being is captured. It is in the will that self and Satan enthrone themselves; it is in the will that the fiercest struggle is carried on. Now, in consecration this citadel is given right over to the Lord. The soul says, "Take my will and make it thine, it shall be no longer mine," and as the soul says take, it gives, and Jesus Christ receives. Then, and not until then, is the life of joy, and peace, and gladness, and power, to which God calls His children, entered. . . .
>
> But someone may say: "I find it impossible to consecrate my will. It is so rebellious it will not put itself under the will of God." If you are not willing to surrender all, are you willing to be made willing? Then make your request known unto God.[2]

That's biblically sound advice. If you're not willing to surrender all, then at least be willing to be made willing. Go to God and say, "I'm willing for you to help me become willing to obey you."

We must come like the anguished father in Mark 9:22–24 whose son was possessed by a demon. "If you can do anything," the man said, "take pity on us and help us."

Jesus said, "Everything is possible for one who believes."

"I do believe," the father said. "Help me overcome my unbelief!"

This father wasn't able to believe. His faith wasn't strong enough—but his obedience supplied what his faith lacked. He was willing to be made willing.

So Jesus rebuked the demon and delivered the boy.

"Help my unbelief. I'm willing to be made willing." That's a prayer I've prayed many times in my life. It's not double-talk. It's absolute honesty in prayer before God.

When our faith is too small, we must offer up our obedience: *Lord, I am handing you the decision-making process for my life. Let your Holy Spirit do whatever he wants. Don't even give me a vote in the matter.* Believe me, God honors this kind of prayer.

When Moses took matters into his own hands and committed murder, God sent him to the University of Faith for forty more years of schooling. Though Moses had already graduated from Heliopolis University with degrees in worldliness and power and arrogance, he needed to study at God's school of higher learning and earn degrees in godliness and servanthood and humility.

As we noted earlier, when Stephen testified before the Sanhedrin, he divided the life of Moses into three stages of forty years each. Stage 1 was in the palace, where Moses learned that he was something. Stage 2 was in the desert with the Midianites, where he learned that he was nothing without God. Stage 3 was when he learned that God is everything.

In the first forty years of his life, Moses believed in Moses. That's why he was so deeply hurt by the rejection of his fellow Hebrews. He fled because he feared the rejection of his Israelite brothers. Where did this fear drive Moses? Into a wilderness of hopelessness and helplessness. What did he have left? Nothing but God.

In the wilderness, Moses learned to believe in God, not in himself. Maybe you can identify with Moses. You might be where he was, in a wilderness of hopelessness and helplessness. You might be saying to God, "Where are you, Lord? I know I disobeyed and ran ahead of your will. I believe you are the God of second chances—but where is my second chance? What's taking so long?"

Here's a vital biblical principle: God is never too late, and God is never too early. He is always right on time. He is working out the circumstances of your life for your good, even if you don't think it's good, even if you don't agree with God's judgment.

Moses fled from Egypt to take refuge in the land of Midian, a desert country, God's school of faith and character. The book of Numbers calls Moses "a very humble man" (12:3), but Moses was not a humble man when he killed the Egyptian, nor was he a humble man when he fled to Midian. God had to send Moses into the desert to teach him humility.

What does the Bible mean when it speaks of the humility of Moses or the humility of Jesus? We tend to think of humility (sometimes called "meekness") as a kind of weakness, a kind of self-effacing bashfulness. When the Bible speaks of humility or meekness, it means "strength under control."

In his early years, Moses had great strength—but his strength was out of control. His strength was subject to his emotions. His strength was not governed by the Spirit of God. Soon we will see how God takes the out-of-control strength of Moses and transforms it into humility and meekness for service to God.

If you are currently enrolled in God's University of Faith, you are going to be greatly encouraged by the rest of Moses's story.

■ QUESTIONS FOR REFLECTION AND DISCUSSION ■

1. Remembering times of great spiritual growth in your life, were they mostly times of testing and adversity—or times of ease? What lessons have you learned about God in times of adversity?

2. Moses had the right motives but took the wrong action when he murdered the Egyptian. Have you ever tried to do God's will in your own way? What did you learn from that experience?

3. God chooses to use broken people for his glory. Can you recall an experience when you were broken for God's glory? Explain. Do you believe God specializes in turning brokenness into beauty? Why or why not?

4. Is there an area of your life in which you struggle to trust God?

5. Even when your faith seems too small, you can still offer God your obedience. Are you able to honestly say, "Lord, I'm willing to be made willing"? Why or why not?

Willingness
obe. God.

Hitting Bottom

Exodus 3–4

In the map room of Southwick House in England, June 6, 1944, the Allied High Command, led by General Dwight D. Eisenhower, faced a decision: proceed with the D-Day invasion—or recall the fleet. The senior commanders around the table voiced their opinions. Some said go; others said abort. The final decision was Eisenhower's alone.

Finally, Eisenhower said, "Let's go." He carried a handwritten note in his pocket as he said those words. The note read:

> Our landings in the Cherbourg-Havre area have failed to gain a satisfactory foothold and I have withdrawn the troops. My decision to attack at this time and place was based upon the best information available. The troops, the air and the

54

Navy did all that Bravery and devotion to duty could do. If any blame or fault attaches to the attempt it is mine alone.[1]

At sunrise, thousands of troops poured from landing craft onto the beaches, braving a hail of bullets and artillery. Within hours, Allied troops had secured eighty square miles of coastline at the cost of ten thousand soldiers dead or wounded. The invasion was costly but successful, and Eisenhower's note, taking full responsibility for failure, was not needed.

Authentic leadership takes responsibility and makes no excuses. But when God appeared to Moses in the desert for the first time, this future leader of the Israelite people gave God four excuses for disobeying God's command.

Moses had fled from Egypt and settled in the desert of Midian. While sitting at a well, Moses saw some shepherds mistreating seven Midianite girls who had come to draw water. Moses stood up to the shepherds and drew water for the girls. Their father was Jethro,[2] a priest of the idol-worshiping religion of Midian. When Jethro heard what Moses had done for his daughters, he gave one of the girls, Zipporah, to Moses in marriage. Moses stayed in Midian and tended sheep for his father-in-law, Jethro.

I believe Moses was a sensitive and emotional man, given to broodings and moods. It's easy to picture him spending those forty years in Midian brooding over being rejected by his people in Egypt. I think I can identify with Moses—at least a little.

When I graduated from seminary and was ordained to the ministry, I worked as an associate at a church led by a very tough minister. He loved God and preached God's Word, yet he had a reputation for being difficult to work with. People warned me to avoid this church and this minister. But I sensed God calling me to work there.

After a year at that church, this man sat me down and said, "Michael, you're not cut out to be a pastor. You're too sensitive and tenderhearted."

The church elders learned of what he had said to me, and they tried to convince me this pastor was wrong, but I took his words to heart. I left the pastoral ministry for a decade. That was my "desert exile" period, and God used that time to teach me that he could use me to advance his kingdom, even though I was at the opposite end of the emotional spectrum from that pastor.

I think Moses may well have been an emotionally sensitive man whose heart was easily bruised by rejection—and by years of unanswered prayer. Moses was God's man, chosen to lead Israel out of slavery. But before God could use him, Moses had to learn to serve in God's way and in God's timing.

The Emotional Brokenness of Moses

Moses had journeyed far from the palace of Pharaoh, far from a world in which people bowed to him and treated him with royal honors. Now, after forty years in the desert, he was just getting over the pain of being spurned by his people. In Midian, his thoughts probably alternated between hope and depression, between concern for his people and resentment over their rejection of him, between wanting to go back to liberate them and wanting to resign from life.

How do I know this? In the Old Testament, people named their children according to their state of mind at the time of the child's birth. If they were in a jovial mood, they would give their children happy, joyful names. If they were in a depressed mood, they would give their children sad, tragic names.

In 1 Samuel 4, the daughter-in-law of Eli the priest was pregnant during a time of war with the Philistines. Word came from the battlefront that Phinehas, the woman's husband, had died in battle and that the ark of the covenant had been captured by the Philistines. When Eli heard the news, he fell, broke his neck, and died. The shock of so much bad news sent Eli's daughter-in-law into labor. She gave birth to a boy and named him Ichabod, meaning "the Glory has departed from Israel." Then she died in despair.

When Jacob's wife Rachel was dying in the pangs of childbirth, she wanted to name the baby Ben-Oni, meaning "son of my trouble," but the baby's father, Jacob, named him Benjamin, "son of my right hand."

In Exodus 2:22, Moses's wife, Zipporah, gave birth to a son, and Moses named him Gershom, saying, "I have become a foreigner in a foreign land." The naming of this baby by Moses tells us that Moses felt alienated from the land of his birth, and he felt alienated in the land of his exile. He was a man without a country—a stranger in a strange land.

Later, Moses will experience healing in his emotions, and Zipporah will give birth to a second son. Moses will name this son Eliezer, which means "God is my helper," and Moses will say, "My father's God was my helper; he saved me from the sword of Pharaoh" (Exod. 18:4).

But before he could experience emotional healing, Moses had to undergo forty years of schooling in the land of Midian, tending his father-in-law's sheep. It was a far cry from the advanced courses in mathematics, military arts, and political science he had studied at Heliopolis University. But the lessons God taught him in the desert were much more meaningful than anything he had learned in Egypt.

The Egyptians worshiped the sun, the moon, and the stars. Moses learned from the One who created the sun, the moon, and the stars. God was preparing Moses, teaching him the character traits he would need to endure the complaining of the Israelites. Moses could never have learned those traits in Pharaoh's palace. He could only learn them through forty years of tending dumb sheep.

Moses's Four Excuses

While leading the flock to the far side of the desert, Moses came to Mount Horeb, "the mountain of God" (Exod. 3:1). There he saw a bush that was on fire but was not consumed. Moses moved closer, and God called to him from the burning bush:

"Moses! Moses!"
And Moses said, "Here I am."
"Do not come any closer," God said. "Take off your sandals, for the place where you are standing is holy ground.

. . . I am the God of your father, the God of Abraham, the God of Isaac, and the God of Jacob." (vv. 4–6)

As Moses quaked in fear, God continued:

I have indeed seen the misery of my people in Egypt. I have heard them crying out because of their slave drivers, and I am concerned about their suffering. So I have come down to rescue them from the hand of the Egyptians and to bring them up out of that land into a good and spacious land, a land flowing with milk and honey. . . . So now, go. I am sending you to Pharaoh to bring my people the Israelites out of Egypt. (vv. 7–10)

Note the irony of Moses's response to the Lord's command. Forty years earlier, a young, arrogant Moses thought he would single-handedly deliver his people from slavery. He murdered the Egyptian slave master, and then he fled and spent forty years in the desert. His dream of being the Hebrew liberator evaporated. His self-confidence hit rock bottom.

Now Moses was right where God wanted him. God is the best bottom-fisher that ever was. God does not despise the brokenhearted. He specializes in recruiting those who have hit bottom. As the psalmist writes:

> My sacrifice, O God, is a broken spirit;
> a broken and contrite heart
> you, God, will not despise. (Ps. 51:17)

God's message to Moses was, "I am sending you to Pharaoh to bring my people the Israelites out of Egypt." How those words must have stung the soul of Moses! God was sending him to Egypt, to the place of his greatest failure and re-gret. With those words, God tore open Moses's emotional wound.

Was God being cruel to Moses? No, but like a compassion-ate surgeon, God was cutting into Moses's soul to remove the cancer of shame and self-reproach within him. God told Moses, in effect, "Go back to Egypt. I want you to deliver my people. You failed before, but this time you will go in my power and my timing—and you will succeed."

Moses responded with excuses:

"Who am I that I should go to Pharaoh and bring the Isra-elites out of Egypt?"

And God said, "I will be with you. And this will be the sign to you that it is I who have sent you: When you have brought the people out of Egypt, you will worship God on this mountain."

Moses said to God, "Suppose I go to the Israelites and say to them, 'The God of your fathers has sent me to you,' and they ask me, 'What is his name?' Then what shall I tell them?"

God said to Moses, "I AM WHO I AM. This is what you are to say to the Israelites: 'I AM has sent me to you.'" (Exod. 3:11–14)

Did you spot the first two of Moses's four excuses? We'll look at each one in detail, and we may find we have some-thing in common with Moses.

If God is calling you to take on a challenge, but all you can think of is past failures—

If God is opening a door for you, but all you can think of is pain and betrayal—

60

If God is urging you to step into the future, but you remain mired in the past—

Learn from the story of Moses.

The First Excuse

Moses said, "Who am I that I should go to Pharaoh and bring the Israelites out of Egypt?" In other words: "I'm nobody, Lord. I blew it once; I'll just blow it again. Find someone else."

Moses didn't misunderstand God's will forty years earlier. God truly did call him to deliver Israel from bondage, but God wanted Moses to do so according to his plan and in his timing. Forty years earlier, Moses had been Mr. Egypt. He had been a big shot, the adopted heir of the pharaohs, the general of the most powerful army in the ancient world. All of that had been stripped from Moses, along with his youthful arrogance. Finally, God could use him.

You may feel inadequate for the challenge God has called you to. That's great news! You're in the same place Moses was when God called him at the burning bush.

God's reply to our excuses is the same as his reply to the excuses of Moses: "I will be with you." I can't read or hear those words, "I will be with you," without an emotional reaction. There have been so many times in my life when I said to myself, "I can't do this. I'm weak. I'm exhausted." And I would hear God speak to me as he spoke to Moses: "I will be with you." And those words gave me the strength to rise up and go forth—not in my own failing strength but in his might.

God gives power to the brokenhearted. God strengthens trembling knees and bent backs. And he has a word for all who feel they can't take another step, who feel they aren't equal to the challenge: "I will be with you." And that's all we need. The only question is, Do you trust the power and might of God?

He has promised, "I will be with you." And he always keeps his promises.

The Second Excuse

Moses made his second excuse to God: "Suppose I go to the Israelites and say to them, 'The God of your fathers has sent me to you,' and they ask me, 'What is his name?' Then what shall I tell them?"

Names are important in the Middle East. Forty years earlier, Moses had been a big name in Egypt. His name had opened doors. His name used to make things happen.

But his own people had rejected him. Pharaoh had pursued him, seeking to execute him for murder. The name of Moses no longer carried clout. It carried a curse. So Moses needed a bigger name than his own, a name with power and authority.

"I AM WHO I AM," said the Lord. "This is what you are to say to the Israelites: 'I AM has sent me to you.'" In effect, God was telling Moses, "I am the eternal God of your forefathers. I'm the God of the past. I'm the God of the present. I'm the God of the future."

If God had said, "I am the God of Abraham, Isaac, and Jacob," he would have been the God only of the past. If he had said, "My name is 'I can,'" he would have been the God only of the present. If he had said, "My name is 'I will,'" he would have been the God only of the future.

But "I am" means "I am the God of the past, the present, and the future." It's no wonder, then, that Jesus—God in human flesh—identified himself to his hearers with such words as "I am the bread of life" (John 6:35), "I am the resurrection and the life" (11:25), "I am the way and the truth and the life" (14:6). "I am . . . I am . . . I am . . ."

This same I AM is the One who spoke to Moses from a burning bush at Mount Horeb in the land of Midian. Without the great I AM, there would be no salvation, no forgiveness of sin, no eternal life in heaven.

The first excuse Moses offered was "Who am I?" The second excuse was "Who are you?" And the Lord answered, "I AM."

The Third Excuse

Moses said, "What if they do not believe me or listen to me and say, 'The LORD did not appear to you'?" (Exod. 4:1).

This is Moses's root problem—he is wallowing in self-doubt, and these emotions are causing him to doubt God as well. He thinks, *I once thought I could be a leader and a liberator, but my own people rejected me. They won't even listen to me.*

God said, "I will be with you," and God even gave Moses his own name to speak. Still Moses doubted. Notice how gently God responds to his fears and doubts. He doesn't scold or condemn Moses. Instead, God gives him three signs with which to convince any doubters.

First sign: God tells Moses, "Throw [your staff] on the ground" (v. 3). Moses tosses his staff—and it becomes a snake. When he picks up the snake by the tail, it becomes a staff again.

Second sign: God tells Moses, "Put your hand inside your cloak" (v. 6). Moses does—and when he takes his hand out of his cloak, it is white with leprosy. When he puts his hand back inside his cloak, the leprosy vanishes.

Third sign: The Lord says, "If they do not believe you or pay attention to the first sign, they may believe the second. But if they do not believe these two signs or listen to you, take some water from the Nile and pour it on the dry ground. The water you take from the river will become blood on the ground."

God patiently answered Moses's third excuse by offering him three convincing signs to validate the authority of Moses.

The Fourth and Final Excuse

Moses saved his biggest excuse for last. He said, "Pardon your servant, Lord. I have never been eloquent, neither in the past nor since you have spoken to your servant. I am slow of speech and tongue" (Exod. 4:10).

In the New Testament, the first Christian martyr, Stephen, stood before the Sanhedrin and said, "Moses was educated in all the wisdom of the Egyptians and was powerful in speech and action" (Acts 7:22). Yet here in Exodus 4, Moses tells the Lord, "I am slow of speech and tongue." Perhaps the emotional shock Moses suffered forty years earlier turned this eloquent public speaker into a stutterer. He lost his glibness and confidence.

So God responds, "Who gave human beings their mouths? Who makes them deaf or mute? Who gives them sight or makes them blind? Is it not I, the LORD? Now go; I will help you speak and will teach you what to say" (vv. 11–12).

Has God finally persuaded Moses to trust him? Moses is out of excuses, but he still refuses to do as God commands. "Pardon your servant, Lord," Moses responds. "Please send someone else" (v. 13).

Moses has a lot of nerve, calling himself a "servant" and calling God "Lord." Moses is a servant who refuses to serve and obey his Lord. He has crossed the line into disobedience and unbelief. So God must shake him up. He tells Moses that the time for excuses is over. It's time for Moses to say, "Yes, Lord."

So God says, "What about your brother, Aaron the Levite? I know he can speak well. He is already on his way to meet you, and he will be glad to see you. You shall speak to him and put words in his mouth; I will help both of you speak and will teach you what to do. He will speak to the people for you, and it will be as if he were your mouth and as if you were God to him. But take this staff in your hand so you can perform the signs with it" (vv. 14–17).

So Moses finally agrees—and obeys.

What Is Your Answer?

Pastor Tommy Hilliker stood in line at a Starbucks in Southern California when he noticed the man behind him. They caught each other's eye, then both looked away. Pastor Hilliker felt God speaking to his heart: *Talk to him.*

He thought, *That's not God speaking to me. That would be too weird to just strike up a conversation with a stranger in Starbucks.* Yet he continued to feel a nudge from God.

Pastor Hilliker ordered his coffee; then the other man ordered his. They waited at the counter for their orders, and the other man's coffee arrived first. The man took the cup, accidentally tipped it, and spilled coffee all over Pastor Hilliker. At that moment, Hilliker wished he'd simply talked to the man as God had urged him.

The man apologized for the spill, then said, "My name is John. Could we talk?"

Hilliker said, "I'm Tommy. Sure, let's sit down."

They took a table and John said, "When I was seventeen years old, I got into a bad car accident and was disabled. Because of my injuries, I died and was resuscitated three times. Now I'm forty years old, and I don't know why I'm here on this earth. Can you help me? Can you tell me? When I saw you in line and I caught your eye, something inside me said, 'You need to talk to that guy.'"

Tommy Hilliker said, "The reason you're still alive is because God doesn't want you to die without him. He wants you to know his Son, Jesus."

"How do I do that? How do I get to know Jesus?"

Hilliker said, "Just say to him, 'Jesus, I need you. I'm asking you right now to come into my life and to save me.'"

So John said, "Jesus, I need you. Will you come into my life and save me?"

And there, at a table in Starbucks, John passed from death to life, from despair to the certainty of a relationship with Jesus Christ.[3]

God calls us to carry out his liberating, saving work among hurting, lost people. He called Moses from the flaming heart of the burning bush. He called Tommy Hilliker from a spilled cup of coffee in a Starbucks. How is God calling you? Are you making excuses? Or are you saying, "Yes, Lord"?

◼ QUESTIONS FOR REFLECTION AND DISCUSSION ◼

1. Moses spent forty years shepherding his father-in-law's flocks, waiting for God to answer his prayers. Do you feel that your prayers go unanswered? What is your response to unanswered prayer?

   a. I'm persevering patiently.

   b. I'm becoming impatient.

   c. I've lost hope.

   d. I'm angry with God.

   e. Other _____

2. God called Moses when he had hit bottom. Moses was broken and had lost his self-confidence. Now God was sending Moses back to Egypt with divine power. Do you identify with Moses? Why or why not?

3. Moses gave God four excuses for not obeying his call:

   a. "Who am I, Lord? I'm nobody."

   b. "What if my people ask who you are? Who are you, Lord?"

c. "What if they don't believe me?"

d. "How can I lead the people if I'm tongue-tied?"

Have you ever made excuses to God? What was the result of making those excuses?

4. What is God calling you to do today? Are you making excuses or saying, "Yes, Lord"?

Confronting the Lie

Exodus 5

"We hold these truths to be self-evident, that all men are created equal, that they are endowed by their Creator with certain unalienable rights, that among these are life, liberty and the pursuit of happiness." This statement from the Declaration of Independence is the principle on which the United States of America is founded. To be an American is to believe in certain self-evident truths.

Today, our culture is coming unraveled because society no longer recognizes commonly held, self-evident truths. As a *Washington Post* columnist declared in 2016, "It's official: Truth is dead. Facts are passé."[1]

Why does our world no longer value truth? One reason is a philosophical movement called postmodernism, which began in the late twentieth century. Postmodernism rejects objective reality and moral absolutes. Postmodern thinkers have replaced the old values with demands for "political correctness" and redefined notions of "tolerance." Christians are expected to tolerate behavior the Bible tells us is sinful, while those who commit such sins have no obligation to tolerate Christians. As one social critic observes:

> There is no mystery that Christianity is unacceptable to the postmodern paragons of tolerance. For the Christian worldview holds that the one and only God objectively intervened (and intervenes) in history and that its truth claims are absolutely valid and open to rational, empirical investigation. Truth, to Christians, is not a function of whatever a person says it is. Nor is religion valid simply because someone affirms it. Postmodernists—those who peddle the euphemisms of tolerance, diversity, openness, multiculturalism, and the rest—view Christianity as inherently in conflict with their subjective assumptions about the world, including their notion that truth itself is just a tool to justify power. . . . Postmodernists fear and oppose those who subscribe to absolute truth.[2]

Postmodern notions of "tolerance" and "political correctness" have become so entrenched in our culture that there is no longer any respect for truth in our media, in academia, or in government. When respect for truth has been discarded, so has respect for the One who said, "I am the way, the truth, and the life."

Too Late?

When Don Shula was head coach of the Miami Dolphins, a reporter questioned the way he corrected a player's mistake in practice. Wasn't he being overly harsh? "We never let an error go unchallenged," Shula said. "Uncorrected errors multiply."

The reporter asked whether it was sometimes best to over-look "small flaws." Shula replied, "What is a small flaw?"[3]

Few leaders today follow the Shula principle—and that includes leaders in the church. Today, we are very tolerant and accepting of so-called small errors, especially errors in our thinking about God, the Bible, and objective truth. And those small errors have multiplied and grown to become towering mountains of delusion and apostasy.

We can't blame the world. If the world believes a lie, that's just the world being the world. But God calls us to be salt and light in this dying world—salt acting as a seasoning and preservative, and light shining as the illumination of God's truth. If the world has become tasteless, corrupt, and dark, it's because we have failed to be salt and light.

If I were to compare my own life with a football game, I'd have to say I'm in the fourth quarter of the game. So, in the closing minutes of this game, I know God is calling me to take a stand, however unpopular, for his truth. He is calling me to fear no one but him, to place nothing above his glory, to seek nothing but his kingdom and his righteousness, to lift up nothing but the cross of Jesus. This stance will not make me popular. But I must not place popularity with men above the truth of God's Word. As the old song reminds us, "Though none go with me, still I will follow; no turning back."[4]

More than a year before the attack on Pearl Harbor, which drew the United States into World War II, General Douglas MacArthur warned, "The history of failure in war can almost be summed up in two words: Too late. Too late in

71

comprehending the deadly purpose of a potential enemy. Too late in realizing the mortal danger. Too late in preparedness."[5]

Is it too late for the church? Is it too late for Western civilization? I pray that we have not idled away the precious time God has given us. I pray it is not too late.

The War of Truth versus Lies

When God set his challenge before Moses, he offered Moses unbelievable power—a power far beyond that of Pharaoh. Even so, Moses felt inadequate and begged God to send someone else. In a speech General Eisenhower gave shortly before the D-Day invasion, he told his troops, "There is no victory at bargain basement prices."[6] Victory is costly. Moses knew that, and he weighed the price of victory—and at first refused to pay the price. He made excuses and asked God to send someone else. Once God had demolished his excuses, Moses knew he had to trust God and pay the price.

When Moses chose to obey God, he placed himself in direct conflict with the king of Egypt. This was not merely a political battle between Egypt and Israel. It was not merely a contest of wills between two leaders. The conflict between Moses and Pharaoh is the same conflict all believers face today—a spiritual battle between the one true God and the false gods of this fallen world; a battle between the God of truth and the father of lies; a battle between the Creator and the great destroyer, Satan.

In Exodus 5, we find Moses and Aaron standing before Pharaoh to confront the oppressive Egyptian government. They tell Pharaoh:

"This is what the LORD, the God of Israel, says: 'Let my people go, so that they may hold a festival to me in the wilderness.'"

Pharaoh said, "Who is the LORD, that I should obey him and let Israel go? I do not know the LORD and I will not let Israel go." (vv. 1–2)

Moses and Aaron tell the king that the God of the Israelites has commanded Israel to take a three-day journey into the wilderness to make sacrifices to God. But the king says, "Moses and Aaron, why are you taking the people away from their labor? Get back to your work!" (v. 4). And he sends Moses and Aaron away.

Then Pharaoh tells the overseers of the slaves: "You are no longer to supply the people with straw for making bricks; let them go and gather their own straw. But require them to make the same number of bricks as before; don't reduce the quota. They are lazy; that is why they are crying out, 'Let us go and sacrifice to our God.' Make the work harder for the people so that they keep working and pay no attention to lies" (vv. 7–9).

Lies? Who is lying in this account? Not Moses and Aaron. Not the Israelites. Not God. Pharaoh himself, who symbolizes Satan, is the only liar in this story. He slandered the Hebrew people as "lazy." He lied about their motive for wanting to worship God. He knew he had made it impossible for the Israelites to meet their quota, yet he ruthlessly heaped the blame on them.

The slave drivers carried out Pharaoh's orders and forced the Israelites to gather straw. Predictably, the Israelites fell further behind in brick production. The Israelite overseers went to Moses and Aaron, saying, "You have made us obnoxious to Pharaoh and his officials and have put a sword in their hand to kill us" (v. 21).

So Moses prayed, "Why, Lord, why have you brought trouble on this people? Is this why you sent me? Ever since I went to Pharaoh to speak in your name, he has brought trouble on this people, and you have not rescued your people at all" (v. 22).

Here we see Moses engaged in a contest of wills—a war between God's chosen man and Satan's representative, a war between God's truth and Satan's lies. Unfortunately, the Israelites are being lured by Satan's lies. We see this same battle between truth and lies in our world today—in our schools and universities, in our news and entertainment media, and in our politics.

But the battle between truth and lies is not fought only in the secular world. The church itself is on the front lines in the war between truth and lies. In January 2017, at an Episcopal church in Glasgow, Scotland, the provost of the church invited a Muslim student to read from the Qur'an. The service marked the Feast of Epiphany, the celebration of the appearance of the Son of God to the world. The student chose to read a text from the Qur'an that specifically and pointedly denies that Jesus is the Son of God.

Hearing of the reading of the Qur'an from an Anglican pulpit, Gavin Ashenden, an Anglican personal chaplain to Queen Elizabeth, resigned in protest so that he could speak out against the blurring of the lines between Christianity and Islam.[7]

When a church invites a Muslim to read falsehoods from the Qur'an as an insult to Christ on a Christian feast day, that church has defected to the enemy. The battle lines between truth and falsehood have been drawn—and those battle lines run right through the heart of every church and every believer. God is calling us to stand for the truth. It may cost us to take that stand, but we must be willing to pay the price.

In Atlanta, the pastor of a huge megachurch told his congregation, "In Sunday School we learned the song, 'Jesus loves me, this I know, for the Bible tells me so.' . . . You grew up, but your faith didn't grow up with you. You grew up, but you outgrew your faith. Your childhood God could not stand the rigors of adulthood, the questions of adulthood."

This pastor went on to say that if the Bible is "the foundation of our faith," then "Christianity becomes a 'fragile house of cards' religion. . . . It is next to impossible to defend the entire Bible. But if your Christianity hangs by the thread of proving that everything in the Bible is true, you may be able to hang on to it, but your kids and your grandkids and the next generation will not."

He cited several parts of the Bible he claims cannot be defended, including Israel's exodus from Egypt under Moses, the collapse of the walls of Jericho in Joshua's day, and the creation and flood accounts in Genesis.[8] This pastor seems unaware that Jesus himself said, "Scripture cannot be set aside" (John 10:35). A false view of Scripture is being preached from the pulpit of one of America's largest megachurches. This church has raised the white flag of surrender to the enemies of the truth.

Sharing the Victory

God demonstrated great patience with Pharaoh in his confrontation with Moses. Yet God also demonstrated his indisputable power. As we will see, God sent ten separate judgments against Pharaoh in a relentless attempt to break Pharaoh's will. Each time, Pharaoh faked a change of heart, only to return to his original stance. No one can accuse God of dealing hastily with Pharaoh.

God could have destroyed the Egyptians and delivered the Israelites with a snap of his fingers. But God chooses to use human beings as his instruments. He chooses to empower his people to stand for the truth. God wants us to share in the victory that is rightfully his alone. On the cross, Jesus destroyed the power of Satan, but he wants us to share in the victory that he purchased with his blood.

We cannot share in the Lord's victory unless we stand firmly for God's truth. Tragically, many who call themselves Christians have surrendered to the enemy without firing a shot. In our eagerness for safety, in our desire to be popular, in our desperate need to "fit in" with the surrounding culture, some have defected to the enemy's camp.

These days, I hear many weak-kneed Christians say, "We shouldn't be so negative and confrontational. We shouldn't always be talking about the things we're against—we need to talk about the things we're for!" But sometimes, in order to talk about what we are for, we have to contrast it with what we are against.

I am for the gospel of salvation by grace through faith in Jesus Christ, the Son of God, who was born of a virgin, who suffered under Pontius Pilate and was crucified, died, and was buried, and who rose again on the third day. I am for the church. I am for the Holy Spirit. I am for the forgiveness of sins. I am for the resurrection of the body. I am for everlasting life in heaven with Jesus.

But there are many people who preach and teach in churches today who are not for those things. They preach a strange, unbiblical, false "gospel." Some preach a social gospel. Some preach that we can discard the Old Testament. Some preach that Jesus is just one of many ways to God the Father—not the only way as Jesus himself claimed in John 14:6.

So in the midst of proclaiming what I am for, I sometimes must state what I am against. And I am against any message or teaching that opposes or undermines the authority of God's Word. It is no sin to confront lies; rather, it is a sin to allow those lies to go unchallenged.

It's certainly possible to confront lies in a sinful way. We must never do so in a spirit of arrogance, bitterness, hatred, or rudeness. We must confront sin and lies firmly, courageously, uncompromisingly, but always in a spirit of humility and love.

You and I must confront Satan by the power of the blood of Jesus Christ. Just as Moses had only one refrain—"Let my people go!"—you and I must have one refrain in our prayers to God as we command Satan, "Let my son or daughter go! Let my spouse go! Let my church go! Let my nation go! By the authority of the blood of Jesus, let them go!"

Are you gripped by a habit or an addiction that gives Satan the keys to your life? Command Satan in Jesus's name, "Let me go!" Is Satan keeping your thoughts mired in bitterness or stuck in a pattern of anger, or are you haunted by guilt or the memory of some injustice done to you? Command Satan in Jesus's name, "Let me go!"

This spiritual principle comes straight from the example of Moses. But I warn you: Satan will respond as Pharaoh responded. The more you command Satan to let you go, the more outraged Satan will become. Like Pharaoh, who repeatedly hardened his heart, Satan may tighten his grip on you at first, hoping you will give up. Or he might leave you alone for a while to lull you into complacency. Then, when you least expect it, he'll attack you again.

Never forget that Satan's fangs were removed at the cross. He can snarl and threaten and tempt and accuse all he wants, but you are safe in the arms of your heavenly Father.

God's Judgment: Already in Motion

Moses could have witnessed Pharaoh's cruelty and said, "Enough! I give up! You can keep the Hebrew people in slavery—just don't make them suffer!" But Moses didn't do that. He could have listened to the accusations of the Hebrew people and said, "Enough! I know I made things worse! I'll stop demanding that Pharaoh let you go." But Moses didn't do that either.

The more pressure Pharaoh applied, the more Moses trusted the promises of God. This doesn't mean Moses never questioned God. Moses did ask, "Why have you brought trouble on this people?" But in spite of his question, he continued to trust God. As Moses's faith grew, Pharaoh's rage increased.

Moses was an emotional, impulsive man, yet he seemed to understand that emotions can change unexpectedly. We can be joyful and enthusiastic one moment and paralyzed with depression minutes later. Our emotions are subject to changes in our circumstances or even hormonal imbalances.

But Moses clung to the promises of God instead of being led by his emotions.

Emulate Moses. Don't give in to feelings. Don't give up on faith. When you come to the end of your rope, tie a knot and wait for God. He is building your faith muscles. He is exposing the lies of sin and Satan while demonstrating his mighty power.

Make no mistake, Satan has one overriding desire: he wants people to worship him instead of God. He achieves this goal by spreading false religions around the world. He sends false teachers with false doctrines to infiltrate the church. Through atheism, secular humanism, philosophical naturalism, pseudoscience, false religion, and on and on, he keeps people ignorant and blind to the truth.

We see Satan's desire to be worshiped in his most audacious statement to the Lord Jesus during the temptation in the wilderness: "All this [all the kingdoms of the world and their splendor] I will give you if you will bow down and worship me" (Matt. 4:8–9). On the cross, our Lord Jesus Christ showed Satan who is truly King. There, Jesus pummeled Satan. No, he didn't finish Satan off. But Jesus is coming back, and Satan knows his doom is certain.

Those who do not worship Jesus with all their heart, mind, soul, and strength leave the door open to Satan's deception. Those who do not worship Jesus as the sovereign King leave space in their hearts for Satan to rule.

Egypt in the time of Moses, the Roman Empire in the time of the early church, and Western civilization today all have much in common. These societies are drenched in religious pluralism and a tolerance for false doctrines and false idols. These societies embrace religious, spiritual, moral, and sexual perversion while persecuting the truth. Inevitably, these societies bring on themselves the judgment of God. I believe God's judgment is already in motion in our world. The signs are everywhere. Our culture is torn by hate, and the love of many has turned cold. Christianity, once the majority worldview, is reviled and mocked in our media and universities. False prophets infest many churches. These trends will grow worse as the day of the Lord's return grows nearer.

"Who Is the LORD?"

I once visited the Room of the Mummies in the Cairo Museum, which had been closed to visitors for many years. My Muslim guide was forbidden to look at the dead bodies in that room, so he said, "As you enter, notice that among all the mummies of the pharaohs in that room, there is one that appears to have been bleached."

I entered, and just as my guide had said, all the mummified pharaohs in that room were dark-skinned but one. After touring the room, I asked my guide who the light-skinned pharaoh was. He said, "That is the pharaoh who your Bible says was drowned with his army in the Red Sea while pursuing the Israelites."

Whenever I hear someone say that the Old Testament accounts cannot be trusted, I think of that light-skinned mummy in the Cairo Museum. It is the mortal remains of the man we read about in Exodus 5.

God was patient and long-suffering with Pharaoh throughout the ten plagues. This same gracious, patient God called Noah to preach repentance for 120 years before the flood finally came. This same God persevered with Israel for three centuries as prophet after prophet warned that God would bring the Babylonians against them if they did not repent. This same God persevered with Israel as Jesus warned Jerusalem not to reject its Messiah. But in AD 70, as Jesus predicted, the Romans demolished the city and the temple. Today, God commands us to call our generation to repentance before it's too late.

When Moses and Aaron first confronted Pharaoh, the Egyptian king said, "Who is the LORD, that I should obey him and let Israel go? I do not know the LORD." It's true. Pharaoh did not know the Lord. He did not know the Lord's justice. He did not know the Lord's power. But he was about to find out.

Do you know the Lord? It's not too late to repent of your sin and receive God's grace. If you have never obeyed the voice of the Lord before, now is the hour. Will you respond?

■ QUESTIONS FOR REFLECTION AND DISCUSSION ■

1. On your job, in your neighborhood, on your campus, or on social media, have you felt the pressure to conform to the world and its corrupt values? Are you influencing the world for God, or is the world pressing you into its mold? Explain.

2. Moses said to God, "Why, Lord, why have you brought trouble on this people? . . . You have not rescued your people at all." In this blunt, honest prayer,

81

is Moses being disrespectful to God? Do you think God welcomed Moses's prayer—or did Moses deserve punishment for it?

3. Has God ever called you to take a risky stand that could cost you your job, a business deal, money, reputation, friendships? How did you respond? What did your decision cost you?

4. Pharaoh told Moses and Aaron, "Who is the LORD, that I should obey him and let Israel go? I do not know the LORD." Do you have friends, family members, neighbors, or coworkers who do not know the Lord? Will you pray for opportunities to tell them the good news of Jesus Christ?

Manifested Power

Exodus 7–10

Kyoto, Japan, is the home of Sanjusangendo Temple, a Buddhist temple built in 1164. It features a hall containing 1,001 hand-carved, gold-overlaid statues from the twelfth and thirteenth centuries. I'm told that each statue is slightly different from the rest so that pilgrims to the shrine can worship the statue that looks the most like themselves. It is a form of self-worship.

I'm reminded of Satan's original lie to Adam and Eve: taste the fruit, disobey God, and your eyes will be opened. You will be like God (Gen. 3:5). It's the oldest lie in the book. Self-worship is the largest religion in the world. It takes many forms but always consists of three ingredients: me, myself, and I.

In ancient Egypt, Pharaoh was viewed as a god, the incarnation of the Egyptian sky god Horus. Egypt was a land of idols, and the pharaohs were believed to be mediators between the Egyptian people and their many gods. When Moses stood before Pharaoh, he stood before a man who considered himself a god, a man who thought himself worthy of worship.

You might say that these idol worshipers aren't responsible for their false beliefs because they had never heard about Jehovah. But Romans 1:20 tells us, "For since the creation of the world God's invisible qualities—his eternal power and divine nature—have been clearly seen, being understood from what has been made, so that people are without excuse."

The Egyptians in the time of Moses had even more reason to believe in the God of the Israelites because (as we are about to see) God performed one miracle after another, right before their eyes. Yet most Egyptians refused to believe (though a small number did convert and join the congregation of Israel).

I have heard people say, "If God would perform miracles today as he did in the Old Testament, people would believe." History proves otherwise. When people are determined to reject God, no amount of evidence will ever change their minds. The problem is not a lack of proof but a stubborn will.

The First Plague

As we look at the first nine judgments God sends against Egypt, you may be surprised to see God's sense of ironic humor at work. You'll see what God means when he says in Exodus 12:12, "I will bring judgment on all the gods of Egypt." The first nine plagues are directed at the gods of Egypt. They are a reminder that God's final judgment is coming against those who ignore God and his Son, Jesus.

In Exodus 7, God tells Moses:

> You are to say everything I command you, and your brother Aaron is to tell Pharaoh to let the Israelites go out of his country. But I will harden Pharaoh's heart, and though I multiply my signs and wonders in Egypt, he will not listen to you. Then I will lay my hand on Egypt and with mighty acts of judgment I will bring out my divisions, my people the Israelites. And the Egyptians will know that I am the LORD when I stretch out my hand against Egypt and bring the Israelites out of it. (vv. 2–5)

God began with a warning and a miraculous demonstration of power. Moses and Aaron did as God commanded. Before Pharaoh, Aaron threw down his staff. The staff became a snake. Pharaoh called his magicians and had them perform the same demonstration with their secret arts. When Aaron's snake swallowed up the snakes of the Egyptians, Pharaoh still refused to believe.

This first demonstration of power was as much for Moses's benefit as for Pharaoh's. Moses's knees were probably knocking, so God taught him a lesson in trading the world's gold for God's glory. Moses didn't reach a place of rock-solid faith all at once. He learned to trust God by stages, just as you and I do.

Next came the first of the ten plagues. The Lord told Moses and Aaron to stretch a staff over the waters of Egypt, and God would turn those waters to blood. Moses and Aaron did as the Lord commanded, and the waters of the Nile turned into blood. The fish died, and the river stank—yet the Egyptians stubbornly refused to heed God's warning.

Growing up in Egypt, I learned that the Nile is the gift of life to Egypt. There is so little rain there that if the Nile suddenly went dry, most of the people would die of thirst in days. The Nile provides drinking water and agricultural irrigation and is Egypt's main artery of transportation and source of fishing. Take away the Nile and Egypt cannot survive.

Osiris, the Egyptian god of fertility, agriculture, and the afterlife, was associated with the annual flooding of the Nile, bringing fertile topsoil to the agricultural region along the riverbanks. There were other gods and goddesses associated with the Nile. The Egyptians made offerings and sacrifices— including human sacrifices—to the gods of the Nile.

God's first judgment humiliated the gods of the Nile by turning the life-giving Nile into a source of horror and death. The waters were cursed for seven days.

Pharaoh begged Moses to pray that the Nile be restored, and Moses did so. But after God answered the prayer of Moses, Scripture records, "Pharaoh's heart became hard; he would not listen to Moses and Aaron, just as the LORD had said" (v. 22).

More Plagues, More Oppression

Exodus 8 opens seven days after God turned the Nile to blood. God tells Moses:

86

Go to Pharaoh and say to him, "This is what the LORD says: Let my people go, so that they may worship me. If you refuse to let them go, I will send a plague of frogs on your whole country. The Nile will teem with frogs. They will come up into your palace and your bedroom and onto your bed, into the houses of your officials and on your people, and into your ovens and kneading troughs. The frogs will come up on you and your people and all your officials."

So Moses told Aaron to stretch his staff over the waters of Egypt, and the frogs came up and covered the land. Why did God send a plague of frogs?

One of the Egyptians' most beloved goddesses was Heqet, the goddess of fertility. Heqet was pictured as a frog because she was identified with the annual flooding of the Nile, which brought fertile soil and frogs far inland. Because of this connection between Heqet and frogs, the Egyptians worshiped frogs.

Here we see God's ironic sense of humor. He says, in effect, "So you worship frogs, do you? Well, here are more frogs than you've ever imagined. Worship these!"

The frogs were everywhere. They hopped into the bowls as the Egyptians made bread and prepared food. They hopped into the Egyptians' beds as they tried to sleep. They squished beneath the Egyptians' chariot wheels. The Egyptian religion didn't allow them to call the exterminator. A devout Egyptian couldn't very well kill the goddess of fertility!

The dilemma was horrifying from the Egyptian point of view. These idolaters were besieged by their own idols. Pharaoh summoned Moses and Aaron and said, "Pray to the

Lord to take the frogs away from me and my people, and I will let your people go" (v. 8). Moses prayed to God, and the Lord did as Moses asked. But as soon as this plague ended, Pharaoh hardened his heart.

The third plague God sent was a plague of gnats (or possibly lice or sand flies). The gnats came out of the ground and afflicted people and animals. They burrowed into the skin, inflicting pain and itching on all, including Pharaoh himself. The plague of gnats was directed at Geb, the Egyptian god of the earth and soil. It was said among the Egyptians that an earthquake was the laughter of Geb. But God's judgment against Egypt turned Geb, the earth god, into an enemy unleashing swarms of gnats on the land.

The royal magicians tried to reason with Pharaoh, calling the plague of gnats "the finger of God" (v. 19). But Pharaoh wouldn't listen. He exhibited a temporary, false-hearted repentance, but neither God nor Moses was fooled.

The fourth plague was beetles. The NIV translation says it was a plague of flies, but I believe beetles is a better translation. The insects swarmed into Pharaoh's palace and across the land. The Egyptians viewed beetles as sacred. God said, in effect, "You like to worship beetles? I'll give you beetles. You and your children will eat with beetles and sleep with beetles."

Pharaoh offered Moses a compromise: "Go, sacrifice to your God here in the land." But Moses refused.

Moses said, "The sacrifices we offer the LORD our God would be detestable to the Egyptians. . . . We must take a three-day journey into the wilderness to offer sacrifices to the LORD our God, as he commands us."

Pharaoh said, "I will let you go to offer sacrifices to the LORD your God in the wilderness, but you must not go very far. Now pray for me." (vv. 26–28)

Moses prayed and God dispersed the flies. But Pharaoh hardened his heart again.

Adopted Idolatry

In Exodus 9, we see the fifth plague, a plague on livestock. The cattle of the Egyptians died, but God spared the Israelites' livestock. Even after this devastating plague, Pharaoh refused to let the Israelites go.

Again God directs his judgment against the gods of Egypt. Apis was a sacred bull worshiped as a god. If you go to the Egyptian city of Luxor and view the temple ruins, you'll see many images of Apis. When a bull died in ancient Egypt, it received an elaborate ceremony and was buried in a vault at the Saqqara necropolis near Memphis. When God struck down the cattle of the Egyptians, he struck down a god.

Many Israelites adopted the idolatry of their Egyptian taskmasters and were neck-deep in the cult of bull worship. In Exodus 32, after God delivered the Israelites from Egypt, they went to Mount Sinai where Moses received the Ten Commandments. While Moses was on the mountain, the people became impatient and reverted to the worship of Apis, the bull god. They pressured Aaron into creating an image of a golden calf, and they claimed that this bull god had brought them out of Egypt. They forgot the God who made the heavens and earth, and they became depraved worshipers of Egyptian idols.

In Exodus 9, God destroyed the Egyptian bull god, but Pharaoh's heart remained hardened. He refused to let God's people go.

The sixth plague was a plague of boils. Moses and Aaron took soot from a furnace and, in Pharaoh's presence, tossed the soot to the wind. Immediately, festering boils broke out on all the Egyptian people and their animals, including Pharaoh himself.

Boils are painful, pus-filled nodules in the flesh, commonly caused by an infection of Staphylococcus bacteria. The boils were all over the bodies of the Egyptians. They couldn't sleep or sit or lie in comfort. They dared not scratch. Even the royal magicians of Egypt were in too much pain to appear before Pharaoh.

There's another irony in this account. It was customary in ancient Egypt for the idol-serving priests to take the ashes of the burnt sacrifices and sprinkle them on the Egyptian worshipers as a blessing. The people were eager to receive this sign of favor from the gods. But in the hands of Moses, those ashes became a curse, not a blessing.

Extraordinary Phenomena

The seventh plague was hail. Again, Moses took the word of the Lord to Pharaoh: "You still set yourself against my people and will not let them go. Therefore, at this time to-morrow I will send the worst hailstorm that has ever fallen on Egypt, from the day it was founded till now. Give an order now to bring your livestock and everything you have in the field to a place of shelter, because the hail will fall on every person and animal that has not been brought in and is still out in the field, and they will die" (vv. 17–19).

Some of Pharaoh's officials believed God and brought their people and animals inside. Others ignored God's warning. When Moses stretched out his hand to the sky, the hail fell—and many Egyptians died. Fields and trees were destroyed throughout Egypt, except in Goshen where the Israelites lived. I call this form of judgment "extraordinary phenomena."

If you've never visited Egypt, you may not realize how extraordinary it would be to experience lightning, thunder, and hail in that land. I was raised in the southern region of Egypt and was eleven years old the first time I saw lightning and heard thunder. The sight and sound of it made quite an impression on me. There was no rainfall that day except in the distance. The first time I experienced rain was when I was an eighteen-year-old student in Cairo. It was a staggering sight—water falling from the sky! I had heard of rain, of course, but I was absolutely amazed to feel rain on my face and arms. During some years, Egypt will get 365 days of sunshine, especially in the middle and southern regions. You can imagine the terror these phenomena struck in the hearts of the Egyptians, including Pharaoh.

The king must have wondered how he was faring in the opinion polls. The people had always looked on the pharaohs as gods. Public opinion was undoubtedly turning against him—and against the entire pantheon of Egyptian gods. The Egyptian sky deities were Horus, god of kingship and the sky, and Nut, goddess of the night sky and stars. Both Egyptian sky deities were useless against God's might.

Again Pharaoh seemed to have a change of heart. He told Moses and Aaron, "This time I have sinned. . . . The LORD is in the right, and I and my people are in the wrong. Pray to the LORD, for we have had enough thunder and hail. I will let you go; you don't have to stay any longer" (vv. 27–28).

Moses said he would pray, but he added, "I know that you and your officials still do not fear the LORD God" (v. 30). And he was right.

A Devouring Plague and a Dark Plague

Exodus 10 introduces the eighth plague—locusts. As instructed by God, Moses and Aaron went to Pharaoh and said:

> Let my people go, so that they may worship me. If you refuse to let them go, I will bring locusts into your country tomorrow. They will cover the face of the ground so that it cannot be seen. They will devour what little you have left after the hail, including every tree that is growing in your fields. They will fill your houses and those of all your officials and all the Egyptians—something neither your parents nor your ancestors have ever seen from the day they settled in this land till now. (vv. 3–6)

Pharaoh's own officials begged him to set the Israelites free. But Pharaoh would only agree to let the Israelite men worship in the wilderness. Against the pleading of his advisors, he insisted on keeping the Israelite women and children as hostages. He tried to bargain with God—but God does not bargain. He demands obedience.

On God's instruction, Moses stretched out his staff over Egypt, and the Lord sent swarms of locusts to cover the ground. The locusts devoured everything the hail had not destroyed.

Again we see God attacking the gods of Egypt. With this plague, God humiliated Nepri, the Egyptian god of grain, and Nepit, the goddess of grain, as well as the other gods who were supposed to protect Egypt from catastrophes. The God of Abraham, Isaac, and Jacob had defeated all the gods of Egypt.

Remember God's promise in Exodus 12:12: "I will bring judgment on all the gods of Egypt. I am the Lord." You might ask, "Why does God need to bring judgment on a bunch of mythical beings who don't even exist?" While it's true that there was no "god of the sky" or "goddess of grain" as the Egyptians imagined, these false gods were fronts for Satan and his demons. When the Egyptians sacrificed to their gods, they were worshiping demons.

Looking out over his devastated nation, Pharaoh again pretended to repent. Moses prayed for the plague to be lifted. But, as Exodus 10:20 tells us, "The LORD hardened Pharaoh's heart, and he would not let the Israelites go."

In Exodus 10, we also encounter the ninth judgment, a plague of darkness. God tells Moses, "Stretch out your hand toward the sky so that darkness spreads over Egypt—darkness that can be felt" (v. 21). Moses stretched out his hand, and all of Egypt was plunged into darkness for three days. If you've ever experienced complete darkness for three minutes or three hours, you know how frightening that can be. But three days! The darkness was so intense, the people couldn't see their hands in front of their eyes.

The Egyptians understood that this judgment was a humiliation of the most important god in their pantheon. Ra, the sun god, had disappeared. By banishing the sun from the sky, God had dealt a crippling blow to the false Egyptian religion.

For three days, no one moved, no one ate, no one could see. It was as if the nation of Egypt had gone blind. Yet God supernaturally provided light in the camp of the Israelites.

Once more, Pharaoh seemed to repent. He told Moses, "Go, worship the LORD. Even your women and children may go with you; only leave your flocks and herds behind" (v. 24).

When Moses insisted the livestock be released as well,

> Pharaoh said to Moses, "Get out of my sight! Make sure you do not appear before me again! The day you see my face you will die."
>
> "Just as you say," Moses replied. "I will never appear before you again." (vv. 28–29)

Though softly stated, Moses's reply sounded ominous.

In this series of nine judgments, God had afflicted everything the Egyptians held sacred. First the river. Then the land. Then the sky. Again and again, the Creator told Egypt that he alone was to be worshiped—not his creations.

Here we see the unity of God's Word. In Revelation, the last book of the Bible, we see a series of future judgments that will be poured out on the world, represented as bowls and trumpets. Each of the judgments of Revelation corresponds to a judgment against Egypt.

Today, as in the day of Moses, the world refuses to listen to the voice of God.

God Does Not Make Deals

God detests cheap repentance, the kind of false repentance demonstrated again and again by Pharaoh. God detests the temporary and insincere "change of heart" we make to get what we want from God. You've heard of a "foxhole conversion" in which a soldier in the heat of battle prays, "God, if you get me through this alive, I'll give up all my bad habits and live for you!" Then, once the shooting stops, the soldier forgets his promise.

With each judgment, Pharaoh experienced a foxhole conversion. He said, "I'll let the Israelites go—at least, the men." Or, "I'll let the Israelites go—as long as their livestock remains in Egypt." He always held something back—and when the crisis was over, he even forgot to keep the halfhearted promise he had made. He thought God could be cajoled and tricked.

Pharaoh didn't reckon with a God who sees the heart. God knew Pharaoh would weasel out of his promises. Nothing Pharaoh did caught God by surprise.

We can't bargain with God or manipulate him with insincere promises. Those who think they can fool God become progressively more self-deluded every time they try. I have seen many people come to a sad end in much the same way Pharaoh did.

God cannot be manipulated. You may think you are getting away with something, but his eyes see everything. He loves you, but he will not allow you to get away with hypocrisy and deceit. We all sin, but if we are sincere in our faith, we will turn back to God in repentance. God loves to hear our prayers of repentance—and he knows if our repentance is sincere or not.

In Luke 11:24–26, Jesus tells a parable that has puzzled many people over the years: "When an impure spirit comes out of a person, it goes through arid places seeking rest and does not find it. Then it says, 'I will return to the house I left.' When it arrives, it finds the house swept clean and put in order." In other words, the house is empty. "Then it [the demon] goes and takes seven other spirits more wicked than itself, and they go in and live there. And the final condition of that person is worse than the first."

Jesus is saying that when an impure spirit (a demon) leaves a person and the Holy Spirit is not invited to come in, there is an empty space within that person. The demon will return, find that life empty, and will fill that space with seven more demons.

The person who cries out, "God, if you just get me out of this mess, I'll change; I'll give up this and stop doing that," may be in more peril than he imagines. If God rescues him but he doesn't sincerely give his life to Christ and receive the Holy Spirit, he leaves himself open to worse tribulations down the road.

God gave Pharaoh many opportunities to repent. Pharaoh kept altering the bargain—just as Satan does in his dealings with us. But Moses would not settle for anything short of total obedience to God. Pharaoh never learned his lesson, but it's not too late for you.

Is God calling you? Come to him in complete surrender.

■ QUESTIONS FOR REFLECTION AND DISCUSSION ■

1. Consider this statement: "When people are determined to reject God, no amount of evidence, not even a miracle, will ever change their minds. The problem is not a lack of proof but a stubborn will." Do you agree or disagree? Explain.

2. Why do you think Pharaoh hardened his heart and refused to let Israel go despite the terrible plagues God sent against Egypt?

3. The plagues against Egypt were God's judgments against the false gods of Egypt. What false gods do we worship today? How should you respond to the idolatry around you?

4. What false gods, if any, do you cling to? How should you respond to the idolatry in your life?

5. Have you ever tried to bargain with God? What was the result of that attempt?

The Firstborn and the Lamb

Exodus 11:1–12:42

On December 7, 1941, the Japanese air force bombed Pearl Harbor. At that moment, the United States and Imperial Japan became locked in a life-or-death struggle. By early 1945, the United States and its allies were closing in on the Japanese mainland. Though casualties mounted on both sides, Japan refused to surrender.

In July 1945, two months after the end of the war in Europe, the Allies issued the Potsdam Declaration, demanding that Japan surrender unconditionally or face "prompt and utter destruction." Japan's leaders ignored the ultimatum. President Harry S. Truman decided that, to avoid millions of deaths in an invasion of Japan, the United States would use a powerful new weapon, the atomic bomb.

On August 6, the United States detonated an atomic bomb over Hiroshima, Japan, and 129,000 souls were extinguished in moments. On August 9, a bomb exploded over Nagasaki, and 226,000 people died instantly. On August 15, Japan surrendered. World War II was over.

We have seen a similar pattern in the book of Exodus. Nine times, God demonstrated his power over the false gods of Egypt. Each time, Pharaoh refused to budge.

So God prepared to deal a blow to Egypt more devastating than all nine previous judgments put together. God's tenth judgment would be the atomic bomb of judgments, bringing devastation and ruin to the heart of Pharaoh himself.

Answering Atheists and Skeptics

As Exodus 11 opens, the Lord tells Moses, "I will bring one more plague on Pharaoh and on Egypt. After that, he will let you go from here, and when he does, he will drive you out completely. Tell the people that men and women alike are to ask their neighbors for articles of silver and gold" (vv. 1–2).

So Moses told Pharaoh about the next judgment: at midnight, the Lord would cause every firstborn son in Egypt to die, but the Israelites would be spared. God had humiliated the entire pantheon of Egyptian gods and goddesses. Now, God would strike a final blow against Pharaoh himself, the self-proclaimed incarnation of the Egyptian sky god Horus—and against Pharaoh's successor, the firstborn prince.

Critics of the Bible have seized on this tenth plague as evidence that the God of the Bible is cruel and unjust. They twist the account of the contest between Moses and Pharaoh to attack our faith. Notice, for example, how atheist spokesman Richard Dawkins mocks God and distorts the details of the account in his 2019 book *Outgrowing God*:

> Pharaoh had been on the point of giving up and letting the Israelites go earlier, and that would have been nice because all those innocent children would have been saved. But God deliberately used his magic powers to make Pharaoh obstinate, so that God could send some more plagues, as "signs" to show the Egyptians who was boss. Here's what God said to Moses:
>
> > But I will harden Pharaoh's heart, and though I multiply my miraculous signs and wonders in Egypt, he will not listen to you. Then I will lay my hand on Egypt and with mighty acts of judgment I will bring out my divisions, my people the Israelites. And the Egyptians will know that I am the Lord when I stretch out my hands against Egypt and bring the Israelites out of it. (Exodus 7:3–5)
>
> Poor Pharaoh. God "hardened his heart" in order to make him refuse to free the Israelites, specifically so that God could do his Passover trick. God even told Moses in advance that he would make Pharaoh say no. And the blameless firstborn children of the Egyptians were all killed as a result. By God. As I said, it's not a pretty story and we can be thankful it never really happened.[1]

Instead of honestly analyzing the account, Dawkins resorts to mockery, demeaning God with phrases such as "his magic powers" and "his Passover trick." Aware that few of his readers will take time to read Exodus 7–11, he makes statements that are careless. There is never any hint that (as Dawkins claims) "Pharaoh had been on the point of giving up and letting the Israelites go earlier." Without question, Pharaoh's repeated offers to free the Israelites were nothing but deceitful ploys.

And what of Pharaoh's hardness of heart? A careful reading shows that there is more to this story than atheists and skeptics admit. In Exodus 7:13, we read that when Moses and Aaron first approached the king, demanding freedom for the Israelites, "Pharaoh's heart became hard and he would not listen." In Exodus 7:22, during the first plague when the Nile turned to blood, "Pharaoh's heart became hard." In Exodus 8:15, "when Pharaoh saw that there was relief, he hardened his heart." In Exodus 8:19, we read, "Pharaoh's heart was hard." In Exodus 8:32, we read, "But this time also Pharaoh hardened his heart and would not let the people go." In Exodus 9:7, after the plague on the livestock, we read, "Yet his heart was unyielding and he would not let the people go."

Six times, Exodus refers to the heart of Pharaoh, but not once in those six passages do we read that God hardened Pharaoh's heart. In each instance, Pharaoh hardened his own heart. Finally, in Exodus 9:12, during the plague of painful boils, we read, "But the LORD hardened Pharaoh's heart and he would not listen to Moses and Aaron, just as the LORD had said to Moses." Only at a point midway through the ten plagues does God fulfill the prediction he made to Moses in Exodus 7:3: "I will harden Pharaoh's heart."

God did not deprive Pharaoh of his free will. The first six times Pharaoh hardened his heart of his own free will, without God's intervention. God gave Pharaoh every opportunity to repent, but Pharaoh made his own willful choice again and again. He was determined to keep the Israelites in perpetual slavery.

The seventh time Pharaoh refused to let the Israelites go, God simply confirmed the decision Pharaoh had repeatedly made. Even so, God still gave Pharaoh one more chance to repent. In Exodus 9:34, after the demonstration of rain, hail, and thunder, Pharaoh "sinned again: He and his officials hardened their hearts." Every time after that, God affirmed the decision Pharaoh had made and he hardened Pharaoh's heart.

In order to make God out to be cruel and unjust, Richard Dawkins has to misrepresent and mock the details of the Exodus account. An honest, objective reading of the text tells a very different story from the Dawkins version.

And what about the accusation by Richard Dawkins that God is cruel and unjust, that "the blameless firstborn children of the Egyptians were all killed" by God? Did God kill the firstborn children of Egypt—or did Pharaoh?

History shows—and the Bible affirms—that evil leaders invariably bring harm to their people. In Matthew 15:14, Jesus calls the evil religious leaders in Israel "blind guides," adding, "If the blind lead the blind, both will fall into a pit." Isaiah writes:

> Those who guide this people mislead them,
>   and those who are guided are led astray. (Isa. 9:16)

Read through 1 and 2 Kings, and again and again you see the wicked kings of Israel and Judah leading their people to death and destruction while dragging their nation down into slavery and oppression. That is why Solomon says:

Like a roaring lion or a charging bear
   is a wicked ruler over a helpless people.
      (Prov. 28:15)

I've heard some people say, "Why punish the entire Egyptian nation? Why didn't God just punish Pharaoh with frogs and flies and beetles and boils and all the rest? Why did the innocent have to suffer?" That question misses the point of the Exodus account. God was not merely judging Pharaoh. He was judging the entire Egyptian system of idolatry. He was demolishing the Egyptian pantheon of false gods. That's why the ten plagues were necessary.

God was not merely trying to pry the Israelites out of Pharaoh's iron grip. He was trying to free the Egyptian people from their satanic religion. He was slaying their gods before their eyes and giving them a chance to believe in the one true God.

And here's the good news that Richard Dawkins and other critics of the Bible miss: many Egyptians were converted to faith in God. Exodus 12 tells us that the Lord "made the Egyptians favorably disposed toward the [Israelite] people" (v. 36), and when the Israelites were free to leave Egypt, "many other people went up with them" (v. 38). In other words, many Egyptians (and possibly other non-Israelites) joined the Israelite community and the Israelite faith. The awesome demonstration of God's power was a mighty form of evangelism, drawing some Egyptians to faith in God.

A Foreshadowing of the Cross

The Passover and the exodus out of Egypt required the shedding of blood—the blood of an innocent lamb. Many people, including many who call themselves Christians, are offended at the shedding of blood. Many apostate preachers and theologians now reject the cross of Christ altogether. For example, some years ago, an interfaith group gathered at the Re-Imagining Conference to "re-imagine" and redefine Christianity. A feminist theologian from Union Theological Seminary in New York, Delores S. Williams, told the group, "I don't think we need a theory of atonement at all. I don't think we need folks hanging on crosses and blood dripping and weird stuff." She added that she believed Jesus didn't come to die for our sins but to show us how to live.[2]

As the apostle Paul writes, "Jews demand signs and Greeks look for wisdom, but we preach Christ crucified: a stumbling block to Jews and foolishness to Gentiles, but to those whom God has called, both Jews and Greeks, Christ the power of God and the wisdom of God" (1 Cor. 1:22–24). And as the writer of Hebrews states, "Without the shedding of blood there is no forgiveness" (Heb. 9:22). Blood atonement is God's idea, not man's idea. We first see this principle at work in the garden of Eden. After Adam and Eve sinned, God killed an innocent animal, probably a lamb, to provide a covering for their shame and nakedness.

God accepted and approved of Abel's sacrifice of a lamb but rejected Cain's sacrifice of grain. When God made the covenant with Abraham, the blood of animals was shed, and God passed through the blood-soaked ground, foreshadowing the cross. And when God stayed the knife-wielding hand of Abraham and spared the life of his son Isaac, God provided a ram as a sacrifice, another foreshadowing of the cross. It is likely that Jesus was sacrificed on that very mountain.

Now in Exodus 12, God directs his people to take action that again foreshadows the cross of Jesus. Every year since the exodus from Egypt, the Jewish nation has celebrated the Passover. The Passover looks to the past and to the future. It points backward to Israel's deliverance from Egypt and forward to the shed blood of Jesus the Messiah.

God gave Israel a set of strict rules for the Passover observance. Each man was to take a lamb for his household—a year-old male without defect, symbolizing the sinless Son of God. The Israelites were to slaughter the lambs at twilight and place some of the blood on the sides and tops of their doorframes, symbolizing the blood-stained cross of Christ. They were to roast the meat over fire, eat it, and be ready to travel. God would slay the firstborn of any household without bloodstained doorposts, but he would pass over any home with blood on the doorposts (hence the feast day called Passover).

So the Feast of Passover was established and has been celebrated every year among the Jews. The Feast of Passover was fulfilled sixteen hundred years after the original event. It is no accident that Jesus celebrated the Passover with his disciples the night before he was crucified. His death on the cross was the event every Passover celebration pointed to.

When God's Son was nailed to the cross and his blood was splashed onto the upright post and crossbeam, the Lamb of God, perfect and without sin, was sacrificed for your sins and mine. From that time, all animal sacrifices have ceased.

How can God accept the sacrifice of animals after the perfect sacrifice of his Son on the cross?

The Old Testament sacrifices are merely symbolic images of the Lamb of God. Once the Lamb himself had been sacrificed on the cross, there was no need for sacrificial animals. That's why John the Baptist declared of Jesus, "Behold, the Lamb of God, who takes away the sins of the world!" (John 1:29 ESV). Animal sacrifices never removed sin. They reminded people of the enormity of sin while pointing them toward a coming Savior. The blood on the doorframe was a foreshadowing of Jesus's sacrifice to come.

The Powerful Message of the Passover

God acted decisively to liberate his people from slavery in Egypt. The death of every firstborn son was a cataclysmic judgment against Egypt. Egyptian society suffered a terrible loss—and many Egyptians rightly blamed Pharaoh for their woes.

The death of the young seems harsh and cruel to our minds—but God had tried every other form of persuasion to no avail. God didn't choose to take the lives of the firstborn sons of Egypt. He gave Pharaoh many opportunities to change his mind. Pharaoh's willful disobedience left God no other option. Only after this horrifying judgment was Israel set free.

In the same way, the death of God's only Son set us free from death and sin. Before Christ came into our lives, we were ruled by a cruel slave master. On the cross, Jesus has set us free from guilt, shame, and the power of sin.

In the first nine judgments God sent against Egypt, he defeated the false Egyptian gods. But in the tenth judgment, God prevented the future god of Egypt—the prince of the house of Pharaoh—from coming to power.

The Passover ceremony is a powerful object lesson that touches not only the mind but also the emotions. You may think that some aspects of this Passover season are cruel, but that is only because sin and Satan are cruel.

God told Israel that on the tenth day of the month of Nisan (around early April on our calendar), the father of the household must choose a lamb without a spot or blemish. The father brings the lamb to the house and lets the children play with it. He allows the family to become emotionally attached to the lamb. Then the lamb is slain. The blood of the lamb is sprinkled on the doorposts, and the lamb is roasted with fire, representing judgment.

The family gathers for the meal, and they eat the lamb together. No doubt, there is sadness on the children's faces as they realize that the meat on their table is the result of the death of an innocent lamb. The father explains that the lamb's death is a sign that God's judgment will pass over their household.

This tenth plague was a judgment against the goddess Isis, protector of children and motherhood. In the previous nine plagues, the Israelites did not have to do anything to be saved. But in the tenth plague, God required the Israelites to take a step of faith and obedience. They had to slay the unblemished male lamb and apply the blood of the lamb to their doorposts. Failure to obey would lead to death. The only protection was the blood of the lamb.

And the only protection you and I have is the blood of the Lamb. As Paul tells us in 1 Corinthians 5:7, "Christ, our

Passover lamb, has been sacrificed." On the night of the first Passover, God's people celebrated their approaching liberation. But on that same night, the homes of the Egyptians were filled with weeping and despair.

This, I believe, is a picture of what the world will be like in the last days. As believers await their liberation from this broken world, unbelievers will mourn and wail. As believers are caught up in the cloud with Jesus, those who have rejected him will await the judgment. Jesus said of the day of his return: "Two men will be in the field; one will be taken and the other left. Two women will be grinding with a hand mill; one will be taken and the other left. Therefore keep watch, because you do not know on what day your Lord will come" (Matt. 24:40–42).

Our mission in these last days is to plead with everyone around us to escape the coming judgment before it's too late. Those who are left behind shall mourn and weep. Those who have rejected the gospel, those who knew of God through his creation and their own consciences but chose to ignore him—they will be without excuse.

But those who love Jesus will be alive with him for ever and ever.

Power in the Blood

It didn't matter whether you were an Israelite or an Egyptian—you would be saved purely on the basis of your obedience. If an Egyptian family sprinkled the blood of a spotless lamb on the doorposts of their home (and some did), they were spared. If an Israelite family ignored the instructions of God, that family would grieve the loss of their firstborn. Those who were judged were not judged because they were Egyptians but because they disobeyed God. Those who were saved were not saved because they were Israelites but because they obeyed God.

The same is true today. Calling yourself a Christian won't save you. Church membership won't save you. Belonging to this or that denomination won't save you. No priest or bishop or pope can save you. Agreeing with a doctrinal statement won't save you. Only the blood of Jesus, sprinkled on the doorposts of your heart, can save you.

As Peter told the Sanhedrin, "Jesus is 'the stone you builders rejected, which has become the cornerstone.' Salvation is found in no one else, for there is no other name under heaven given to mankind by which we must be saved" (Acts 4:11–12). The cross devastates human pride and arrogance. The cross devastates human effort. The cross devastates our self-willed notion that we can save ourselves. That's why the Bible speaks with one voice from cover to cover, saying, "Without the shedding of blood there is no forgiveness [of sin]" (Heb. 9:22).

Today, many churches have removed hymns that speak of the blood of Jesus. They think they are "updating" the Christian faith and making it more appealing, but they are doing Satan's bidding. Satan doesn't want to hear people singing, "There is power in the blood," or "Nothing but the blood of Jesus," or "There is a fountain filled with blood." Victory over Satan is found in the blood of the Lamb.

When you place yourself under the blood of Jesus, Satan will flee. When you place yourself under the blood of Jesus, temptation will fall. When you place yourself under the blood of Jesus, sin will be conquered. When you place yourself under the blood of Jesus, victory will be yours. There is power in the blood of Jesus.

Please understand. The blood of Jesus is not a magical formula to use in vain repetitions. But when you claim the power of the blood, you choose to walk moment by moment in that power. Then you will find power over addiction, power over temptation, and power for serving and ministry.

When you walk by the power of the blood of Jesus, you join the multitudes in heaven who say:

> To him who sits on the throne and to the Lamb
> be praise and honor and glory and power,
> for ever and ever! (Rev. 5:13)

■ QUESTIONS FOR REFLECTION AND DISCUSSION ■

1. Have you ever experienced a hurt or a setback in life that made you question God's fairness and love? Explain your answer.
2. In the account of God's dealings with Pharaoh, God applies steadily increasing pressure on Pharaoh while giving him multiple opportunities to repent. Does God still deal this way with rebellious people? Why or why not?
3. Some Egyptians were converted to faith in God as a result of seeing God's power in action. Has God done a powerful work in your life? Do you use that personal story in your witnessing?

4. Paul writes in 1 Corinthians 5:7, "Christ, our Passover lamb, has been sacrificed." Does the story of the first Passover strengthen your confidence in proclaiming the cross of Christ in your Christian witness? Why or why not?

Faith—or Fear?

Exodus 14:1–18

It was known as "The Invincible Armada," a fleet of 130 ships that set sail from Corunna, Spain, in May 1588. The armada boasted more than 2,500 artillery pieces, 8,000 sailors, and 20,000 soldiers. King Philip II of Spain sent the armada to overthrow Queen Elizabeth I and restore Catholic rule in England.

When the Spanish ships reached England's southern coast, they faced a small force of English ships commanded by Sir Francis Drake and the Earl of Nottingham. The English navy put up a furious fight. The armada lost several ships to English cannons, then retreated to the coast of Calais, France.

The night of July 28, the English navy filled eight "fireships" with tar, pitch, gunpowder, and sulphur, then guided them toward the armada. Just after midnight, sailors set the ships ablaze and jumped overboard. Eight fiery unmanned ships sailed toward the armada, sped along by the wind and tide. The blazing ghost ships filled Spanish hearts with terror.

The panicked Spanish sailors cut their anchor cables and set sail in confusion. Ships collided like bumper cars. The English fireships didn't set a single Spanish ship on fire—but they did send the armada fleeing in disarray.

At dawn, the English attacked the armada off the French port town of Gravelines. In a furious sea battle, the English ships sent the demoralized armada fleeing north. The so-called Invincible Armada was buffeted by storms and depleted by hunger and illness. Many ships foundered on the Irish coast.

By October, surviving ships of the armada limped home to Spain. Half the ships were lost and 15,000 Spanish sailors and soldiers had perished at sea.[1] The defeat of the Spanish armada signaled the collapse of the Spanish Empire. The armada was not defeated by enemy forces or storms. It was defeated by fear the night Spanish sailors saw fiery ships bearing down on them out of the night.

Fear can turn certain victory into immediate surrender. Fear can topple an empire and change history. Fear can rob a Christian of joy and power. The moment you take counsel from your fears instead of your faith, defeat is bound to follow.

Faith and fear are mutually incompatible. When we stop advancing in faith, we retreat in fear. If we are not ruled by faith, we will be imprisoned by fear.

Dr. E. Stanley Jones was a Bible-believing missionary in India. He has been called "the Billy Graham of India." He once wrote:

I am inwardly fashioned for faith, not for fear. Fear is not my native land; faith is. I am so made that worry and anxiety are sand in the machinery of life; faith is the oil. I live better by faith and confidence than by fear, doubt and anxiety. In anxiety and worry, my being is gasping for breath—these are not my native air. But in faith and confidence, I breathe freely—these are my native air. A Johns Hopkins University doctor says, "We do not know why it is that worriers die sooner than the non-worriers, but that is a fact." But I, who am simple of mind, think I know. We are inwardly constructed in nerve and tissue, brain cell and soul, for faith and not for fear. God made us that way. To live by worry is to live against reality.[2]

Fear is the number one enemy of our Christian witness because it prevents us from talking to other people about Christ. Satan loves to trap us in prisons of fear.

Israel Panics

In Exodus 12, after countless Egyptian households have lost a firstborn son, a defeated Pharaoh summons Moses and Aaron. "Leave my people, you and the Israelites!" Pharaoh moans. "Go, worship the LORD as you have requested. Take your flocks and herds, as you have said, and go." Then Pharaoh adds a strange request: "And also bless me" (vv. 31–32).

We don't know why Pharaoh made this request. We can only speculate. Perhaps Pharaoh, being an idolater who worshiped many gods, wanted to add the powerful Hebrew God to the list of those he worshiped. He knew that Moses was

God's representative on earth, so perhaps he asked Moses to put in a good word for him with the God of Israel.

Whatever Pharaoh may have meant when he asked for this blessing, we can be sure that Pharaoh had not experienced a true conversion. He still followed his own false gods, and he would soon go back on his word. He would send his army out to re-enslave the people of Israel.

In Exodus 8:28, after the plague of flies, Pharaoh said to Moses, "Pray for me." And Scripture records that Moses prayed for the plague to end, and God dispersed the flies. But in Exodus 12, there's no hint that Moses blesses Pharaoh. And why should he bless Pharaoh? Pharaoh has never kept his word. Why bless an unrepentant deceiver?

The Egyptian people urged the Israelites to pack up and go. "Otherwise, . . . we will all die!" (v. 33). The Egyptians were so eager to send the Israelites on their way that they even gave them clothing and jewelry.

In Exodus 14, the people of Israel suffer a paralyzing attack of fear—just when their deliverance is at hand. Ten times, God has defeated the false gods of Egypt. Ten times, God has punished Pharaoh while sparing the people of Israel. Now the Israelites can finally leave Egypt and journey to the promised land. Pharaoh has not merely let the Israelites go—he has ordered them out of his kingdom.

So the Israelites leave Egypt and make camp between Migdol and the Red Sea. But when word reaches Pharaoh that they have left, he and his officials change their minds: "What have we done? We have let the Israelites go and have lost their services!" (v. 5).

Pharaoh gathers more than six hundred of his best charioteers, and they set off in pursuit of the Israelites. Before long, the Israelites see a vast cloud of dust approaching. Scripture records that the Israelites "were terrified and cried out to the LORD" (v. 10).

Whenever we face an apparent impossibility, we will hear three voices. First, we'll hear the voice of Satan saying, "Give up! Surrender! You can't win!" Second, we'll hear the voice of human logic saying, "Stand still! Freeze! This is an impossible situation, and anything you do might make it worse!" Third, if we are attuned to the voice of God, we'll hear him saying, "Trust me! Be of good courage! Follow me!" Those three voices can be heard in Exodus 14.

The terrified Israelites speak the words of Satan. Seeing the approaching Egyptians, they berate Moses with words of defeatism: "Was it because there were no graves in Egypt that you brought us to the desert to die? What have you done to us by bringing us out of Egypt? Didn't we say to you in Egypt, 'Leave us alone; let us serve the Egyptians'? It would have been better for us to serve the Egyptians than to die in the desert!" (vv. 11–12).

Moses answers the people with words of human logic: "Do not be afraid. Stand firm and you will see the deliverance the LORD will bring you today. The Egyptians you see today you will never see again. The LORD will fight for you; you need only to be still" (vv. 13–14). These are paralyzing words—don't move, stand still.

Next, we hear God telling Moses, "Why are you crying out to me? Tell the Israelites to move on. Raise your staff and stretch out your hand over the sea to divide the water so that the Israelites can go through the sea on dry ground. I will harden the hearts of the Egyptians so that they will go in after them. And I will gain glory through Pharaoh and all his army, through his chariots and his horsemen" (Exod. 14:15–17).

The Israelites wanted to go back, Moses wanted to stand still, but God said, "Forward march!" Question: Why did the Israelites want to crawl back to their Egyptian slave camps? Answer: fear. Craven, cowardly, cringing fear.

But let's not be too hard on the Israelites. In those circumstances, fear is a natural response. They saw Pharaoh's mighty army behind them, the Red Sea in front of them, and not much of a future in between. I'm not sure my faith would have fared any better.

God has given us this account not to portray the Israelites as people of little faith but to show us that we can trust God even in our impossible situations.

Panic Leads to Lying

The Israelites "were terrified and cried out to the Lord." Prayer is always the right thing to do in an impossible situation. But sometimes people do the right thing for the wrong reason. The Israelites didn't cry out to God in faith. They cried out in unbelief. They thought God had abandoned them. They shouted at God but had no faith he would hear them.

I have an inkling of what the Israelites felt as they cried out to God. I've known situations where I thought God had abandoned me. In those times, I felt not only fear but despair. But God did not abandon me, just as he did not abandon the Israelites.

It's natural to be fearful at times. It's natural to be anxious as you scale Mount Impossible. Fear is a God-given emotion designed to protect us from doing foolish and dangerous things. But how we respond to fear determines whether we will become a victim of fear or a victor over our fears.

In their panic, the Israelites turned against their leader. They sarcastically berated Moses, saying in effect, "Weren't there enough graves for us in Egypt? Is that why you brought us out into the desert to die?" Egypt was famed for its graves. In fact, Egypt was proud of its graves. There were dead pharaohs entombed in pyramids across the land. There was heavy irony in the words of the frightened Israelites. In times of panic, people often turn against their leaders.

Frightened people often misrepresent the past. They want to blame someone else for their woes, even if it means rearranging the facts of history. The Israelites tell Moses in so many words, "Didn't we tell you to leave us alone in Egypt? Didn't we tell you we were better off as slaves? But you had to stir up the Egyptian hornets' nest, and now we're all going to die!"

Had the Israelites told Moses they wanted to live as slaves in Egypt? There's no account of it in previous chapters. Who in their right mind would prefer slavery to freedom? Who would say, "I just love making mud bricks all day while the Egyptians flog our backs"?

In 2018, the Barna Group conducted a survey among Christians that found that less than three-fourths of Christians believe they have a responsibility to "always speak the truth" and "demonstrate morality" in the workplace. Why do only three-fourths of Christians feel bound by biblical morality and honesty? Why isn't that number 100 percent? The survey also found that only 58 percent of Christians feel they have a responsibility to perform "excellent work to glorify God."[3]

When Christians feel so little responsibility to be honest and moral, what can we expect of the secular world? When God is evicted from public life, the truth is replaced by lies. The Israelites panicked, attacked Moses, and lied to him. Panic is a state of extreme fear and unbelief. Fear throws faith out the window—and when faith goes, morality and integrity go as well.

Authentic Faith Doesn't Stand Still

If the panic-stricken Israelites had gotten their way and returned to Egypt, they would have nullified God's promise to Abraham. They would have prevented the conquest of the promised land. There would have been no kingdom of Israel under David and Solomon, no great prophets such as Isaiah, Jeremiah, Ezekiel, and Elijah. And there would have been no human lineage of Jesus the Messiah.

Whenever we act out of fear instead of faith, we foreclose all that God wants to do for us. How many times has God opened a doorway of opportunity—but you refused to walk through it? How many times has he called you to a life of freedom—but you said, "No, I want to remain a slave"?

How many times has he called you to share Christ with a friend or neighbor, to throw off the chains of a bad habit, to volunteer to serve the poor or sick, to speak out for the oppressed? How many times has God wanted to bless you, but you insisted on your own timetable and expectations? How many times have you heard the voice of God saying, "Go forward! Trust me!"—but you retreated instead?

I can find no instance in Scripture where God blessed anyone for retreating. In the story of Lot's escape from the destruction of Sodom, the angel told Lot and his family to look forward and not look back. Lot's wife disobeyed and was transformed into a pillar of salt.

At Kadesh Barnea, Moses sent a dozen men to spy out the promised land. Ten of the twelve spies returned with fearful reports and recommended retreat. Two of the spies, Joshua and Caleb, wanted to obey God and take the land. The doubters won the debate—and God caused the doubters to wander aimlessly for forty years.

Remember the prophet Jonah? God commanded him to preach repentance to the people of Nineveh. Jonah refused to go forward with God. He ran in the opposite direction. God chastened Jonah with a violent storm and a three-day stay in the belly of a fish.

In Luke 9, Jesus invited two men to follow him. Each man had his own excuse for delaying. One wanted to bury his dead father. The other wanted to say goodbye to his parents and siblings. Jesus said, "No one who puts a hand to the plow and looks back is fit for service in the kingdom of God" (v. 62). These words sound harsh—but this is the truth straight from the lips of Jesus. Satan will tell you to go back, but God says, "Go forward!"

Moses did his best in a stressful situation. The Egyptians were coming fast behind them, the sea blocked their way forward, and the Israelites were shouting insults at him. So he said, "Do not be afraid. Stand firm and you will see the deliverance the Lord will bring you today."

Standing still may be better than turning back, but it's not good enough for God. By standing still, Moses was at least trusting God to come to their rescue. He was saying, in effect, "Don't give up hope. Just wait—God will get us out of this." But God had not called the Israelites out of Egypt to merely stand still. He had called the Israelites to action.

Many Christians think they can stand still in their faith, but faith must move forward. Faith means moving beyond our comfort zone. Faith means investing in God's will and trusting him to pay the dividends. Standing still is not an option. You must move forward with God or fall backward.

The one thing I fear in my church and in our related organizations is complacency. Not lack of money. Not lack of attendance. Not success or failure. Complacency. I worry that people will choose paralysis over moving forward with God. They will choose the status quo over the adventure of faith.

As the world grows increasingly more hostile to faith, as persecution increases, we will find ourselves in a situation much like Moses and the Israelites, with their backs to the Red Sea and all the wrath of Egypt bearing down on them. I fear that our churches and Christian ministries will hunker down like Moses and say, "Everybody keep calm! The Lord will rescue us—just don't move!"

God says to us, as he said to the Israelites, "Why are you crying out to me? Move!" God wants us to pray—but prayer is no substitute for action. God wants us to pray—but we can pray and move at the same time. God wants us to pray—but prayer should prompt us to take risks, not take cover. There is a time for praying on our knees—and there is a time for praying on the run.

In the mid-1980s, I prayed for nearly two years that God would bring The Church of The Apostles into existence. I prayed for clear signs of God's leading. I prayed for wisdom and direction. I prayed and prayed—but I wasn't taking action. Why not? I was apprehensive; I feared making a mistake. God had answered my prayers, and I should have launched out in bold faith. But I held back.

God sent a man to me who said, "Michael, I sense the Lord saying that the time for praying and waiting is past. It's time to trust God and allow the Spirit to give birth to this church." He was right. We held our first worship service soon after that.

Prayer must be accompanied by action. Pray for your financial problems and debts—but cut your spending and increase your giving to God. Pray for your health issues—but follow your doctor's orders. Pray for your neighbors—then go talk to them about Jesus. Pray for your country—but make sure you take time to vote, contact your representatives, and speak out for your faith and values.

Pray—and act. Pray—and risk. Pray—and obey.

When you go forward, God will part the sea for you. When you go forward, God will bless you. When you do your part, God will do his part. When you have done everything possible, God will do the impossible.

■ **QUESTIONS FOR REFLECTION AND DISCUSSION** ■

1. Do you agree that faith and fear are mutually incompatible? Why or why not?

2. Recall a time when you faced a seemingly impossible situation. Did you hear a voice saying, "Give up"? A voice saying, "Stand still"? A voice saying, "Trust God and keep moving forward"? Which voice did you obey? What was the result?

3. Have you ever felt that God abandoned you in a time of crisis? What was the outcome of that crisis? What lessons did you learn?

4. Recall a time when you prayed for an important issue in your life. Did you combine your prayer with action? What lessons did you learn about prayer?

Wandering from the Truth

Exodus 14:19–31

Fulton J. Sheen was a Catholic bishop and an Emmy-winning television preacher. He recalled an incident when he was in Philadelphia to speak at Town Hall. He decided to walk there instead of taking a taxi, but he soon got lost.

He went to a group of teenagers on the street corner and asked, "Can you please tell me the way to Town Hall?"

A boy gave him directions, then asked, "What are you going to do there?"

"I'm going to deliver a lecture."

"On what?"

"On how to get to heaven."

"To heaven?" the young man said. "You don't even know how to get to Town Hall!"[1]

When we follow God, we may not know the way ahead, but we know he will lead us where he has promised. When we wander from God and his truth, we leave ourselves open to calamity.

After leaving Egypt, the Israelites followed a pillar of cloud, the visible sign of God's presence. When the Israelites saw the army of Pharaoh pursuing them, the cloud moved from in front of the Israelites and stood between the Egyptians and the Israelites. Throughout the night, the cloud brought darkness to the Egyptians and light to the Israelites.

Moses stretched his hand out toward the Red Sea, and the Lord sent a fierce east wind to force the waters back and turn the seabed to dry land. The wind blew throughout the night, and the Israelites walked on dry ground with two walls of water towering over them on either side. The Egyptians pursued them into the seabed during the last watch of the night, between 3:00 a.m. and 6:00 a.m., and the Lord threw the Egyptians into confusion.

Then God told Moses to stretch his hand out toward the sea. When he did, the walls of the sea collapsed, and the army of Pharaoh—and Pharaoh himself—drowned in the violent waters. There were no Egyptian survivors. Witnessing this sight, the Israelites put their trust in God and his servant Moses. At that moment, the Israelites were ready to follow God anywhere.

But it was only a matter of time before they would wander away from God and his truth.

The Pillar of Cloud

In the Old Testament, the Hebrew word *'anan* that is translated "cloud" in English appears twice in Exodus 13: "By day the LORD went ahead of them in a pillar of cloud to guide them on their way and by night in a pillar of fire to give them light, so that they could travel by day or night. Neither the pillar of cloud by day nor the pillar of fire by night left its place in front of the people" (vv. 21–22).

This Hebrew word also appears three times in Exodus 14. For example, in verse 19 we read, "Then the angel of God, who had been traveling in front of Israel's army, withdrew and went behind them. The pillar of cloud also moved from in front and stood behind them." As you picture this scene, you're probably wondering what this cloud is all about.

It was like no other cloud the Israelites had ever seen. It was not the sort of cloud we see in the sky. It was not made of water vapor. The Bible calls it a cloud because it had a cloudlike appearance, but our language has no word to adequately describe it.

On July 16, 1945, when the first atomic bomb was tested in the desert in New Mexico, observers described the explosion as a "mushroom cloud." What those observers saw was neither a mushroom nor a cloud. They called it a cloud because it was billowy like a cloud, and they compared it to a mushroom because of its shape. When our language lacks the words to describe what we see, we do the best we can with the inadequate words we have.

The Exodus "cloud" was not a true cloud. It possessed a will of its own. It protected the Israelites from the heat of the sun by day, and it lit up the sky at night. It gave light to the Israelites as they crossed the Red Sea, and it gave darkness to confuse the pursuing Egyptians.

The pillar of cloud is revealed in the New Testament as the Holy Spirit of God. The "angel of God" in verse 19 is the preincarnate Lord Jesus Christ. The Holy Trinity was actively protecting God's people as they marched from slavery to liberty.

When you receive Jesus as your Lord and Savior, the Holy Spirit—the same Spirit who led the people of Israel and stood between the Israelites and their enemies as a pillar of cloud—comes to live in you. And when you walk in obedience to him, that same Spirit fills you more and more each day.

In the New Testament, the Holy Spirit is often called "the Paraclete." The word *paraclete* comes from the Greek word *paraklētos*, which combines two Greek words, *para-* ("alongside") and *kalein* ("to call"). The Greek word is often translated "Comforter" in English, but the Spirit's role is much greater than merely comforting us when we are downhearted.

The word was originally used in the Greek military, and it referred to a warrior. Greek soldiers went to battle in pairs so that when the enemy attacked, the warriors could stand back-to-back and cover each other's blind spot. A soldier's fighting partner was called a paraclete, one who was called to be alongside in battle. That is the role the Spirit played as a pillar of cloud before the Israelites, and that is the role the Spirit plays in your life and mine today.

Jesus loves us too much to allow us to face life's battles alone. He loves us too much to leave our backs unguarded. He loves us so much that he sent us a partner who guards our blind side in battle. Because Jesus gave the Holy Spirit to you and me, we should never feel isolated or unprotected. That is the Lord's promise to us. Hours before he went to the cross, Jesus told his disciples—and he told you and me—"And I will ask the Father, and he will give you another advocate [*paraklētos*] to help you and be with you forever—the Spirit of truth. The world cannot accept him, because it neither sees him nor knows him. But you know him, for he lives with you and will be in you" (John 14:16–17).

Right on schedule, on the day of Pentecost, the Holy Spirit came to the church to dwell permanently with all believers. Everyone who trusts Jesus as Lord and Savior, everyone who walks in obedience, everyone who eagerly awaits his return has the Holy Spirit living within. If you belong to Jesus, the Holy Spirit is your Paraclete, the warrior who has your back.

Protection, Presence, and Provision

Evangelist Dwight L. Moody once preached a powerful sermon on the Holy Spirit. After the service, a man went up to the evangelist and said, "Mr. Moody, you speak as if you had a monopoly on the Holy Spirit."

"No!" Moody said. "But I do trust the Holy Spirit has a monopoly on me."[2]

May the same be said of you and me! If you are a follower of Jesus Christ, then the Holy Spirit lives in your life. You have all of the Spirit you will ever need. The only question is, Does the Spirit have all of you?

Today, the Holy Spirit is invisible, but in the time of Moses, the Spirit was manifested as a pillar of cloud. That cloud—the Holy Spirit—was given as a sign of God's protection, God's presence, and God's provision. The Spirit performed the same functions in the life of Israel that he performs in our lives today: protection, presence, provision.

The Spirit protected the Israelites. Without the pillar of cloud going before them, they never would have reached the promised land. The cloud protected them from their human enemies. The cloud protected them from the natural dangers of the wilderness. The cloud protected them from the broiling daytime temperatures and the bone-chilling desert nights.

When God the Son gave his children the Holy Spirit, he gave the Spirit in abundance, so that no one could say, "I don't have the protection of the Holy Spirit" or "I don't have the gifts of the Holy Spirit" or "I don't have the presence of the Holy Spirit."

The only time you don't experience the Holy Spirit in you and around you and alongside you is when you quench the Holy Spirit, as Paul writes in 1 Thessalonians 5:19. How do you quench the Holy Spirit? By premeditated disobedience to the Word of God and deliberate sin against God.

In ancient Israel, the cloud was the sign of God's presence with the people. In Exodus 19, God spoke from the cloud when he gave Moses the Ten Commandments. In Exodus 33, God spoke from the cloud in the tent of meeting. In Numbers 12, God spoke from the cloud in judgment against those who rebelled against Moses's leadership.

From the cloud, God saw everything. Through the Holy Spirit who dwells in the believer, God watches every word we speak. God knows every thought we think. God observes our actions and reactions. God is aware of every emotion and desire we feel. How our lives would change if we had a deeper awareness of the presence of God's Spirit in our lives.

In ancient times, when a landowner agreed to sell a parcel of property to a buyer, the seller dug up a piece of turf, wrapped it in the buyer's cloak, and handed it to him. This action symbolized the fact that the land now belonged to the new owner. When the parcel of land being sold was farm-land, the landowner broke a twig from a tree and handed it to the buyer to assure the new owner that all the fruit of the trees on that land now belonged to him. When there was a house on the land, the owner handed the buyer the key to the house to symbolize the transfer of ownership. The new owner had not yet taken physical possession of the land, the farm, or the house, but symbols changed hands to show that the property was under new ownership.

The Holy Spirit plays much the same role in our lives today. God has given us, his children, an inheritance of heaven. We do not yet enjoy the bounty of heaven, and we don't yet live there. But God has given us the Holy Spirit as an assurance of his continual presence in our lives. The Holy Spirit is the turf of our inheritance. The Holy Spirit is the twig from the plentiful tree of life. The Holy Spirit is the key to our eternal mansion.

In Old Testament times, the Holy Spirit did not live con-tinually with his people. Instead, the Spirit came upon cer-tain individual people to accomplish certain specific tasks for a limited period of time. The Holy Spirit did not come to dwell in believers until Acts 2, when the Spirit came upon the church at Pentecost.

The Army of God

In Exodus, the pillar of cloud is a visible symbol of God's presence as well as God's protection. But the pillar of cloud is also a visible symbol of God's provision.

The word *provision* is a meaningful word compounded from a prefix and a noun: *pro* ("ahead") and *vision* ("seeing"). Provision means seeing ahead, looking forward, such as foreseeing a need and taking action to meet that need. The Holy Spirit stands outside of time and can see the future as easily as we remember the past—and the Spirit can provide whatever we will need in the future. An excellent example of the Holy Spirit's provision for the Israelites is found in the book of Numbers:

> On the day the tabernacle, the tent of the covenant law, was set up, the cloud covered it. From evening till morning the cloud above the tabernacle looked like fire. That is how it continued to be; the cloud covered it, and at night it looked like fire. Whenever the cloud lifted from above the tent, the Israelites set out; wherever the cloud settled, the Israelites encamped. At the LORD's command the Israelites set out, and at his command they encamped. As long as the cloud stayed over the tabernacle, they remained in camp. When the cloud remained over the tabernacle a long time, the Israelites obeyed the LORD's order and did not set out. Sometimes the cloud was over the tabernacle only a few days; at the LORD's command they would encamp, and then at his command they would set out. Sometimes the cloud stayed only from evening till morning, and when it lifted in the morning, they set out. Whether by day or by night, whenever the cloud lifted, they set out. Whether the cloud stayed over the tabernacle for two days or a month or a year, the Israelites would remain in camp and not set out; but when it lifted, they would set out. At the LORD's command they encamped, and at the LORD's command they set out. They obeyed the LORD's order, in accordance with his command through Moses. (Num. 9:15–23)

Picture this scene. Imagine you are the head of an Israelite household. You and your family follow the cloud when it moves. Why has God called you and the other Israelites to get up and move? Perhaps some warlike enemy force is coming, and you must get out of their way. Or perhaps a natural disaster is coming or perhaps God has reasons that are beyond human understanding. In any case, if the pillar of cloud moves, you must move.

Question: Do you think the Israelites rejoiced that the cloud was leading them? Absolutely not. They grumbled and complained because the leading of the cloud caused uncertainty and unpredictability in their lives. And they didn't merely grumble about the cloud. They grumbled about their leader, Moses. They would have gladly fired Moses and elected his weak-willed, compromising brother, Aaron, as his replacement.

The Israelites couldn't understand why the cloud moved when it did, why it stopped, or why it sometimes delayed for weeks or months before resuming its movement. They couldn't understand the mind of the Spirit of God. But if they could have understood, they'd have known that every start and stop had a divine purpose. Sometimes the purpose was to save the Israelites from dying in the desert, whether from heat, dust storms, enemies, or marauders.

Through the cloud, God protected the Israelites and provided for them. But that's not all. Through the cloud, God also disciplined the Israelites, transforming them from an unruly mob into an organized army of God, conditioned and trained to conquer the promised land.

Now, if you're like many Christians, you may not enjoy being led by the Holy Spirit. And you certainly don't enjoy the disciplining of the Holy Spirit. A part of you may be saying, "Lord, I want to lead my own life my own way. I want to be like my worldly neighbors. I want to make my own selfish plans and set my own self-centered goals. I want wealth and status and pleasure and all the same things my neighbors want. I don't want to feel the conviction of the Holy Spirit when I sin or when I misuse my money, time, and talent."

We have all felt that way at times. But the Holy Spirit leads you, convicts you of sin, and disciplines you out of love for you. God is preparing you to reign and rule the universe with him. Jesus said, "But very truly I tell you, it is for your good that I am going away. Unless I go away, the Advocate [the Holy Spirit] will not come to you; but if I go, I will send him to you. When he comes, he will prove the world to be in the wrong about sin and righteousness and judgment" (John 16:7–8).

"Lead On, Lord!"

In our fallen humanity, we want to go our own way, do our own thing, gratify our own desires. We love God's grace, but we don't want his discipline in our lives. But God didn't save us from our sin so we could go on sinning. He called us to serve him, to be soldiers in his army. Planet Earth is enemy-held territory, and God has called us to take this territory for his kingdom, just as the Israelites were called to take the promised land in his name. To accomplish our mission, we need to cooperate with the Holy Spirit as he trains us for the spiritual battle.

When the Spirit calls you, what will you say? The only rational response is, "Lead on, Lord. I'm yours to command."

I'm told that certain early Native American tribes had a rite of passage for boys who had reached young manhood. At age thirteen, the boy learned hunting, fishing, and scouting skills, and once he was considered ready, he underwent a final test.

The boy was blindfolded and led into a dense forest to spend the night alone. The night sounds of the forest would fill the boy with dread. This was the domain of the wolf, the bear, and the snake. Could he defend himself? Would he even survive the night?

After what probably seemed like an eternity, dawn broke. The first rays of sunlight filtered into the forest. The boy looked up and saw the figure of a man silhouetted against the morning light—the silhouette of his father. All night long, the boy's father had stood guard over the boy, bow and arrow in hand, ready to protect him from danger—

But the boy didn't know it.

All night long, he had been as safe as if he were home. Though he felt abandoned, he was never alone. He needed to face his fears and prove to himself that he could survive the loneliness and the dark, but his loving father made sure that no harm came near.

You may feel alone right now. You may think God has abandoned you.

But the Holy Spirit is present in your life, providing and protecting, even when you can't sense him. He is your Paraclete, your warrior. He has your back.

When he calls, "Follow me," what will you say? Don't ignore him, reject him, quench him, or grieve him. Say the only rational thing you could possibly say: "Lead on!"

■ QUESTIONS FOR REFLECTION AND DISCUSSION ■

1. Have you felt tempted to wander from God? Who or what brought you back?

2. In John 8:31–32, Jesus says, "If you hold to my teaching, you are really my disciples. Then you will know the truth, and the truth will set you free." What teaching is Jesus talking about? Have you tested this principle in your own life?

3. How does the presence of the Spirit in your life change your outlook? How does his presence influence your decisions and actions?

4. Have you identified your spiritual gifts? Have your Christian friends ever told you that they see certain spiritual gifts in you? How are you using the gifts the Spirit has given you?

The Danger
of Discontentment

Exodus 15:22–16:10

Author Bob Perks tells how he came upon the title of his book, *I Wish You Enough*. He was near the security gate at an airport when he overheard a father and daughter saying their goodbyes. The daughter was departing, the father was staying behind, and from the way they talked, it seemed they expected to never see each other again.

"I wish you enough," the father said, hugging her.

"Your love is all I ever needed, Daddy," she said. "I wish you enough too."

Then she went through the gate and was gone. The father took a seat next to Perks and looked out the window. Then he turned and said, "Did you ever say goodbye to someone knowing it would be forever?"

The two men talked, and Perks learned that this father knew he was nearing the end of his life. His daughter lived so far away that she would probably not return before he died. Perks asked what the man and his daughter meant by "I wish you enough."

The man said it meant "My wish for you is that you will always have enough to live a contented life." Then he recited, "I wish you enough sun to keep your attitude bright. I wish you enough rain to appreciate the sun more. I wish you enough happiness to keep your spirit alive. I wish you enough pain so that the smallest joys in life appear much bigger. I wish you enough gain to satisfy your wanting. I wish you enough loss to appreciate all that you possess. I wish enough 'Hellos' to get you through the final 'Goodbye.'"

Then, with tears in his eyes, the man got up and walked away, leaving Bob Perks to ponder.[1] We would do well to ponder too. You and I are richly blessed in so many ways. But do we have enough? Or are we discontented?

Writing for *Psychology Today*, Dr. Steve Taylor observed that psychological research shows that gaining greater wealth and possessions often leads to greater discontentment: "In general, lottery winners do not become significantly happier than they were before. . . . Extremely rich people—such as billionaires—are not significantly happier than others. Studies have shown that American and British people are less contented now than they were fifty years ago, although their material wealth is much higher."[2]

These insights into human nature are not surprising to followers of Jesus. As the Lord told the Samaritan woman at the well, "Everyone who drinks this water"—the world's water—"will be thirsty again, but whoever drinks the water

137

I give them will never thirst. Indeed, the water I give them will become in them a spring of water welling up to eternal life" (John 4:13–14). The more you drink of the world's water—worldly ideas, worldly values, worldly goals—the thirstier and more discontented you'll become. The more you have, the greater your expectations will be. The greater your expectations, the greater your dissatisfaction. That's why possessions lead to discontentment.

That's how fallen human nature operates (the Bible calls our fallen nature "the flesh"). We are never content with what we have. We want more and more and more.

Like a Seesaw

When we first believed in Jesus as our Lord and Savior, God implanted his divine nature in us. We didn't achieve instant moral perfection, but we began a lifelong process of gradually becoming more and more like Christ. As the apostle Paul explains, "For those God foreknew he also predestined *to be conformed to the image of his Son*, that he might be the firstborn among many brothers and sisters" (Rom. 8:29, emphasis added). We are learning to subdue our fallen, fleshly nature, including our tendency to be discontented with what we have.

Discontentment leads to discord. This is true whether that discontentment erupts in a family, a church, or a nation. Many in the church today are infected with discontentment, which leads to complaining, envy, and dissension as discontented Christians battle other discontented Christians for status and power. As Christians have become more affluent, as small churches have grown into megachurches with huge budgets, the danger of discontentment in the church has grown.

The more you have, the more you want—and the more discontented you become. This is true even when you receive a gift. When Jesus fed the five thousand, there were probably complainers who said, "He gave us fish, but no tartar sauce? And where's the butter for this bread?"

I have found that my own level of discontentment is in inverse proportion to my level of gratitude. A complaining attitude is the opposite of a thankful attitude. The relationship of discontentment to gratitude is like a child's seesaw. When thankfulness goes up, discontentment goes down—and vice versa. Thankful people are not complainers, and complaining people are not thankful. It's impossible to say, "Thank you, Lord, for my blessings," while also saying, "Life is so unfair! Why does everything bad always happen to me?"

I have lived in many countries and many cultures, and I have met both immensely wealthy people and people who are extremely poor. I've been impressed by the fact that an attitude of gratitude has nothing to do with one's economic class or possessions. I've visited mansions filled with bitterness and ingratitude, and I've visited tin shacks filled with joy and thankfulness. Some of the most thankful people I've met had no worldly goods at all.

In Exodus 15, we see that the more the Israelites had, the more they wanted—and the more discontented they became:

> Then Moses led Israel from the Red Sea and they went into the Desert of Shur. For three days they traveled in the desert without finding water. When they came to Marah, they

could not drink its water because it was bitter. (That is why the place is called Marah.) So the people grumbled against Moses, saying, "What are we to drink?"

Then Moses cried out to the LORD, and the LORD showed him a piece of wood. He threw it into the water, and the water became fit to drink.

There the LORD issued a ruling and instruction for them and put them to the test. He said, "If you listen carefully to the LORD your God and do what is right in his eyes, if you pay attention to his commands and keep all his decrees, I will not bring on you any of the diseases I brought on the Egyptians, for I am the LORD, who heals you."

Then they came to Elim, where there were twelve springs and seventy palm trees, and they camped there near the water. (vv. 22–27)

The more the Israelites saw of God's miraculous and protective hand, the more they expected from God—and the more they complained. They had started as slaves, making bricks out of mud under the stinging lash of the slave masters. God had set them free. Yet whenever a problem arose, great or small, from Egyptians in chariots to bitter water, the Israelites complained against God and his servant Moses. In their ingratitude, they forgot the miraculous things God had done.

Unreasonable, Ungrateful, Unbelieving

The Israelites were characterized by three traits. They were unreasonable, ungrateful, and unbelieving. By studying the negative example of the Israelites at that crucial moment in history, we can learn how God wants us to respond to the crises in our own lives. We can see how to become reasonable, thankful, faithful servants of God.

Reason Is a Virtue

First, these murmurers and complainers were unreasonable. They were unreasonable because they complained to Moses, who had no power of his own. They turned on Moses as if he was personally responsible for making the water bitter. They forgot who Moses was and the sacrifice he had made for them. As we read in Hebrews 11: "By faith Moses, when he had grown up, refused to be known as the son of Pharaoh's daughter. He chose to be mistreated along with the people of God rather than to enjoy the fleeting pleasures of sin. He regarded disgrace for the sake of Christ as of greater value than the treasures of Egypt, because he was looking ahead to his reward" (vv. 24–26).

Moses turned his back on the gold of Egypt to identify with the suffering of his people. The story of Moses is not a rags-to-riches story but a riches-to-rags story. As the adopted grandson of Pharaoh, Moses was accustomed to seeing the common people bow before him. Yet he turned his back on wealth and glory in order to serve God.

Did the people respect Moses in his leadership role? Did they appreciate the personal sacrifices he had made? They did not. They berated him and complained about his decisions. Chronic complainers are, by nature, unreasonable people. They don't care about the truth or evidence or logic.

This was true of the Pharisees in the time of Jesus. They complained about everything Jesus did—not because he violated the Scriptures but because his wisdom exposed their corruption. He used rational arguments to refute their criticism, but they didn't learn from him or change their ways when he proved them wrong. Instead, they were filled with a murderous and unreasoning hatred. A reasonable person would have listened to the words of Jesus and said, "You make a lot of sense. I need to give that some thought." But the Pharisees responded by plotting to kill him.

When Jesus healed on the Sabbath, they opposed him and condemned him instead of being thankful that people were being healed. When Jesus presented evidence that he was the long-expected Messiah, they dismissed the evidence without a moment's consideration. They failed to recognize the authority of his words. He attracted great crowds with his teaching, but instead of learning from him, they envied his popularity and hated him all the more.

Complainers and discontented people are unreasonable. They respond emotionally and angrily, not logically. You can't reason with such people.

Reason is a virtue. It's one sign of being Christlike. One of the ways we show we are becoming conformed to the image of Christ is by our growth toward becoming reasonable, rational people.

An Attitude of Gratitude

One day in the 1970s when I lived in southern California, I was driving home to Pasadena. I had been teaching a Bible class at a church in Van Nuys, and I felt I had done a terrible job. My self-esteem was at rock bottom, and I was berating myself. As I drove, I turned on a Christian radio station, and

I heard a preacher delivering an inspiring message. Within moments, I realized that God had chosen this preacher to speak directly to my heart.

He talked about the joy of the Lord. His words rebuked me and blessed me at the same time. His message went something like this:

> Christian, why are you downhearted? Why are you feeling low? How can you not be joyful? You may say, "Brother, you don't know how sick I am" or "Brother, I just lost my job today" or "Brother, I've just lost someone I dearly love." I know that hurts. But you still have reason to be joyful! You can be joyful because of your salvation. You can be joyful because you have been snatched from the jaws of the devil. You can be joyful because you are saved from hell. Even if a mosquito bites you, there's reason to be joyful and you can sing, "There is power in the blood"! Whenever you feel downhearted, thank God for all the reasons you have for joy.

As I listened, I laughed and cried. I prayed as I drove, and I asked God to forgive me for allowing my pride to steal my joy. That lesson has stuck with me through the years. Whenever I get downhearted, I know it's time to go to God in gratitude and ask him to restore my joy.

A spirit of thankfulness enables us to face life with a realistic and positive perspective. A complaining attitude is an ungrateful attitude. Ungrateful people all have three things in common: They have a selective memory. They have a short attention span. They focus on partial truth rather than the whole truth.

We see this principle at work in the lives of the Israelites. Only a few weeks had passed since God delivered the

143

Israelites from slavery in Egypt. They had seen the Lord's miraculous power. They had seen how God divinely humbled the most powerful nation on earth. But in Exodus 16, we encounter this scene of grumbling and complaining:

> The whole Israelite community set out from Elim and came to the Desert of Sin, which is between Elim and Sinai, on the fifteenth day of the second month after they had come out of Egypt. In the desert the whole community grumbled against Moses and Aaron. The Israelites said to them, "If only we had died by the LORD's hand in Egypt! There we sat around pots of meat and ate all the food we wanted, but you have brought us out into this desert to starve this entire assembly to death." (vv. 1–3)

The Israelites were nostalgic for fine Egyptian cuisine—but they forgot that the Egyptians only fed the Israelites "pots of meat" so they could work hard the following day. The Israelites remembered the food in Egypt but forgot the marks of the whips on their backs. Worst of all, they forgot the miraculous deliverance of the Lord.

The lesson is clear: the cure for complaining is an attitude of gratitude. Instead of keeping score of our grievances and complaints, we need to count our blessings every day. No matter how bad our troubles may seem, it's not hard to find blessings to be thankful for.

The Bible treats the sin of ingratitude very seriously. The apostle Paul observes that a lack of thankfulness to God inevitably leads to deeper and darker sins: "For although they knew God, they neither glorified him as God nor gave thanks to him, but their thinking became futile and their foolish hearts were darkened. Although they claimed to be wise, they became fools and exchanged the glory of the immortal God for images made to look like a mortal human being and birds and animals and reptiles" (Rom. 1:21–23).

The widespread decline of thankfulness in our culture has produced a decline of civility across our civilization. That's why Paul writes that ingratitude is one of the signs of the end times: "But mark this: There will be terrible times in the last days. People will be lovers of themselves, lovers of money, boastful, proud, abusive, disobedient to their parents, ungrateful, unholy" (2 Tim. 3:1–2).

God is patient with ungrateful people. He's been patient with me. He was patient with the people of Israel, providing manna from heaven and sweet water in the desert. Though God is patient with our ingratitude, we shouldn't mistake his patience as a sign that God is soft on sin. In the book of Numbers, we see how God, after enduring the complaining of the Israelites, finally responds:

> They traveled from Mount Hor along the route to the Red Sea, to go around Edom. But the people grew impatient on the way; they spoke against God and against Moses, and said, "Why have you brought us up out of Egypt to die in the wilderness? There is no bread! There is no water! And we detest this miserable food!"
>
> Then the LORD sent venomous snakes among them; they bit the people and many Israelites died. The people came to Moses and said, "We sinned when we spoke against the LORD and against you. Pray that the LORD will take the snakes away from us." So Moses prayed for the people.
>
> The LORD said to Moses, "Make a snake and put it up on a pole; anyone who is bitten can look at it and live." So Moses made a bronze snake and put it up on a pole. Then

when anyone was bitten by a snake and looked at the bronze snake, they lived. (Num. 21:4–9)

God sent the snakes among the people not to punish them but to bring them to their senses—and it worked. The people who had spoken against God went to Moses in contrition and repentance. God, in his mercy, provided the bronze snake as a source of healing and forgiveness. Jesus said that the bronze snake was a prophetic symbol of his crucifixion (John 3:14).

Our loving Father has saved us from the pit of hell, from eternal damnation, from the punishment we rightfully deserve. He has provided the solution to our sin, including the sin of ingratitude.

Keep Believing

People who grumble and criticize are in a state of unbelief. We see this in the lives of the Israelites. God had sent plague after plague against Egypt until—at last—Pharaoh finally agreed to let God's people go. The Israelites had watched these displays of God's power from the sidelines—ten miracles, one after another. There are few greater blessings in life than true freedom—and God had blessed them by liberating them from slavery.

Yet every time a challenge arose, the Israelites said, "Where is God now? What has he done for us lately?"

You'd think that, after all the miracles the Israelites had witnessed, they would have a faith that moves mountains, a faith no obstacle could shake. But the moment they had to skip a meal or deal with a disappointment, they exhibited unbelief.

I'm not condemning the Israelites or criticizing them from a sense of moral superiority. Had I been one of the people following Moses in the wilderness, I probably would have exhibited unbelief as well. Unbelief is not an Israelite trait— it's a human trait. No matter how many times God has demonstrated his power and provision in our lives, we are still prone to complaining and unbelief.

We all experience doubt from time to time. When we allow doubt to linger in our thoughts, we place ourselves in spiritual jeopardy. Every time we exercise our faith muscles by trusting God, our faith grows stronger.

Are you waiting for God to fulfill a promise? Are you waiting for him to deliver you from your circumstances? Are you waiting for him to provide for your needs? Ask God to keep your lips from complaining. Trade grumbling for gratitude.

God's delays do not mean denial. Keep trusting him. Keep believing in him. Keep thanking him. Then prepare to receive his blessings.

■ **QUESTIONS FOR REFLECTION AND DISCUSSION** ■

1. As you think back over your life, do you feel contentment with what God has provided for you—or discontentment?

2. In the never-ending war between the flesh and the spirit in your life, do you sense that the flesh is winning—or the spirit?

3. After all Moses had done for the people, they did not respect his leadership role. Have you ever seen this kind of ungrateful disrespect for leaders? Have you taken a stand to defend a leader you felt was unfairly treated?

4. Do you agree that reason is a virtue? Have you ever experienced a time when reason and logic became a hindrance to your faith? Read John 8:31–32. What is the best way to sort truth from falsehood?

5. Are you waiting for God to fulfill a promise? What steps can you take to keep from complaining while you wait?

Victory through Surrender

Exodus 17:8–16

Columnist Dennis Prager tells about a thirteen-year-old boy who played in a youth league baseball game. By the ninth inning, his team was ahead 24 to 7. Then the boy's father noticed the scoreboard abruptly changed to 0 to 0.

After the game, the father asked an official what was wrong with the scoreboard. Answer: nothing. The coach of the winning team had asked for the score change. Parents from the losing team begged the winning coach to make the change so their boys' feelings wouldn't be hurt. Did those parents really think their kids would forget they were losing 24 to 7? Prager concluded:

> It is unwise to the point of imbecilic to believe that the losing boys were in any way helped by changing the score. On the

contrary, they learned lessons that will hamper their ability to mature.

They learned that someone will bail them out when they feel bad. They learned that they do not have to deal with disappointment in life. . . . They learned that their feelings, not objective standards, are what society deems most important. . . .

At the same time, the boys on the winning team learned not to try their best. Why bother?[1]

This incident is a microcosm of what is happening across our society. Everybody's a winner. Everyone gets a trophy. Every student gets an A. There are no losers and no winners.

But in the real world, there *are* winners and losers. No one gets a trophy for just showing up. You must compete to win the prize. As Paul writes:

Do you not know that in a race all the runners run, but only one gets the prize? Run in such a way as to get the prize. Everyone who competes in the games goes into strict training. They do it to get a crown that will not last, but we do it to get a crown that will last forever. Therefore I do not run like someone running aimlessly; I do not fight like a boxer beating the air. No, I strike a blow to my body and make it my slave so that after I have preached to others, I myself will not be disqualified for the prize. (1 Cor. 9:24–27)

In the war between good and evil, there are winners and there are losers.

Retired NBA executive Pat Williams tells a story from his days as general manager of the Atlanta Hawks. In 1971, Atlanta's roster included future Hall of Famer "Pistol Pete"

Maravich. The team was coached by Cotton Fitzsimmons. As the season began, the Hawks quickly piled up losses at home and on the road. Fitzsimmons tried many ways to motivate his players, without success.

One night, Fitzsimmons told his players, "I want you to pretend you're the greatest basketball team in the world. And I want you to pretend that this game is for the NBA championship. And I want you to pretend that instead of a three-game losing streak, we're on a three-game winning streak. Now go get 'em!"

That night, the Hawks suffered one of their worst defeats ever.

After the game, Maravich told Fitzsimmons, "Cheer up, Coach. Just pretend we won!"[2]

There is no pretending in spiritual warfare. When we storm the gates of hell, we must be armored for battle—or we'll become casualties. Those who pretend there is no winning or losing in a spiritual battle will find themselves in a world of hurt.

Some pretend that the war between the spirit and the flesh does not exist. Some even pretend that Satan doesn't exist. But those who follow the Lord Jesus know the spiritual war is real. Only unconditional obedience to him guarantees victory. Partial obedience, selective obedience, or occasional obedience will lead to defeat.

The Ceaseless Struggle

In Exodus 17:8–16, a tribe called the Amalekites attacks Israel at a place called Rephidim. Moses sends his top general,

Joshua, to lead a counterattack. "Tomorrow," Moses tells Joshua, "I will stand on top of the hill with the staff of God in my hands" (v. 9).

Joshua leads his troops against the Amalekites while Moses, Aaron, and Hur climb to the top of the hill. As long as Moses holds his hands high in prayer, the Israelites win. Whenever he lowers his hands, the tide of the battle swings in favor of the Amalekites. Soon, Moses's arms grow tired, so Aaron and Hur stand on either side of Moses and hold his arms steady until sunset, when Joshua's forces finally overcome the Amalekite army.

Moses then builds an altar and names it "The LORD is my Banner," saying, "Because hands were lifted up against the throne of the LORD, the LORD will be at war against the Amalekites from generation to generation" (v. 15).

These days, we hear people talk about "an existential threat"—a threat to the existence of a nation or a culture. The Amalekites posed an existential threat to the Israelite people. The Amalekite tribe was so ruthless that forty years later when Moses was about to die, he told the people, "Remember what the Amalekites did to you along the way when you came out of Egypt. When you were weary and worn out, they met you on your journey and attacked all who were lagging behind; they had no fear of God" (Deut. 25:17–18).

If Pharaoh and his army represent Satan, then the Amalekites represent the flesh. In Galatians 5:17, Paul tells us that every believer possesses two opposing natures, the flesh and the spirit: "For the flesh desires what is contrary to the Spirit, and the Spirit what is contrary to the flesh. They are in conflict with each other, so that you are not to do whatever you want." The New International Version capitalizes *Spirit*, meaning the Holy Spirit. But I believe Paul speaks of the conflict between our flesh and our regenerated spirit, which we received at conversion.

In Romans 7, Paul expresses near despair when he thinks of the war between his flesh and his spirit—yet he does not give up because the power of God works within him:

> So I find this law at work: Although I want to do good, evil is right there with me. For in my inner being I delight in God's law; but I see another law at work in me, waging war against the law of my mind and making me a prisoner of the law of sin at work within me. What a wretched man I am! Who will rescue me from this body that is subject to death? Thanks be to God, who delivers me through Jesus Christ our Lord!
>
> So then, I myself in my mind am a slave to God's law, but in my sinful nature a slave to the law of sin. (vv. 21–25)

Paul knew he could not win the battle in his own strength. He concluded that victory comes from total obedience to God. Anything less leads to defeat. Victory comes not from what we do but from the One we depend on. Victory comes not from our ability but from our availability.

When Christ comes into our lives, he gives us a new nature—but the old nature does not die. It battles for mastery. So the Christian life is a struggle, and it's a struggle we cannot win in our own strength. But God, through the indwelling Holy Spirit, has given us the power to conquer our fallen flesh—not once and for all but moment by moment—as we live in reliance on him.

Prayer and Action

Why do I say that Pharaoh and his armies symbolize Satan while the Amalekites symbolize the flesh? The people of Egypt were total strangers to Israel, a foreign civilization, just as Satan, a nonphysical, spiritual being, is a total stranger to the human race. But the Amalekites were genetically related to Israel. The Amalekites traced their ancestry to Esau, the brother of Jacob, whom God renamed Israel. The Amalekite descendants of Esau were related to the descendants of Jacob by blood—yet the hostility between these two tribes went back to the contention between Esau and Jacob over the birthright from their father, Isaac.

Satan is our external spiritual enemy; the flesh is our internal enemy. Satan attacks from the outside, but the flesh is part of us. Just as Jacob and Esau had the same father and mother but conflicting loyalties, our flesh and our spirit spring from our common humanity, but their loyalties are at war. Jacob and the regenerated Christian spirit are loyal to God. Esau and the fallen flesh are loyal to the self.

Our new nature wants to please the Lord. Our old nature wants to please the self. The new nature is loyal to Christ. The old nature wants to run wild, without moral boundaries. The new nature is guarded by the Holy Spirit and guided by the Word of God. The old nature is ruled by self-destructive appetites.

The Amalekites attacked Israel because they had heard of the great things God did for the Israelites in liberating them from slavery in Egypt. Hearing all that God had done, the Amalekites were filled with envy and set out to destroy God's people.

As soon as Moses saw the army of the Amalekites massing on the horizon, he knew there were two things he had to do. First, he had to go to a high place and seek the only power that could give him the victory—the power of God. Second, he had to send the best he had onto the battlefield—that was Joshua.

Just as Jesus said we are to both watch and pray, Moses looked to both God and the battlefield. He received wisdom from God, and he sent his strongest general to the battlefield. When we are under attack by the flesh, we must get on our knees—then rise up and go into battle. We spend time studying God's truth—then we stand firm for the truth on the battlefield.

Today, we see a dangerous division among Christians. Some "progressive Christians" are only interested in activism. They are very busy with a social and political agenda they have mistakenly labeled "the social gospel." They have lost faith in salvation and the life to come, so they're focused on good works in the here and now. They believe in action—but action alone won't achieve victory. Action must be teamed with prayer.

There are others who only pray and never act, and they use prayer as an excuse for not going out onto the battlefield. They do not witness to others, they do not feed the hungry, they do not reach out to widows and orphans and the poor. They just pray. But God calls us to combine prayer with action.

The lesson of Exodus 17 is that victory requires both prayer and action—in fact, two forms of action. The three secrets to victory over the flesh are kneeling in prayer, standing (first form of action), and waving the flag (second form of action).

155

The Importance of Kneeling

We don't need to physically get on our knees to pray. Kneeling is a posture of reverence for the Lord, and many people feel that kneeling puts them in a prayerful mindset. True enough—but we can pray in any posture: with our hands raised to God, with our hands on the steering wheel, or with our feet in motion as we run from trouble.

How did Moses pray in this account? He lifted up his staff to the Lord. This is an expression of total dependence on God. So when I use the term *kneeling* to signify prayer, I'm saying that true victory over the flesh requires that we surrender to God in prayer, regardless of our actual physical posture.

The practice of kneeling in prayerful surrender may have come from a commonly observed scene in the ancient Middle East—the image of a camel kneeling to be loaded with goods. When the camel stands at full height, it cannot be loaded. People can't reach its back. Only by kneeling in submission can the camel take on its burden.

For the believer, kneeling is a posture that says, "Load me, Lord, with your blessings. Load me with your strength. Load me with victory. Load me with challenges and tasks too, Lord, because I am here to serve you."

During production of the 1959 motion picture *Ben-Hur*, actor Charlton Heston spent many hours practicing for the big chariot race. When he felt he had achieved some competence as a chariot driver, he went to director Cecil B. DeMille and said, "I think I can drive the chariot all right, Cecil, but I'm not at all sure I can actually win the race." DeMille replied, "You just stay in the race, and I'll make sure you win."[3]

In the same way, God told Moses in so many words, "Raise your hands in a posture of surrender, and I will make sure you win." Prayerful submission to God is the secret to victory over the flesh.

The Importance of Standing

In order to win the battle over the flesh, we must stand together in unity. God responds to unity in prayer. That's why Jesus said, "For where two or three gather in my name, there am I with them" (Matt. 18:20). And that's why Jesus, hours before the cross, prayed "that all of them may be one, Father, just as you are in me and I am in you. May they also be in us so that the world may believe that you have sent me" (John 17:21).

When Joshua went to fight the battle, the future leadership of Israel stood on that battlefield. Moses did not give God the leftovers, the inferior, the second best. He sent his top general, Joshua, to fight. Moses gave Israel's all for the battle.

Meanwhile, Moses stood in prayer on the hilltop with his hands lifted in intercession. But he could not persevere in prayer by himself. He needed Aaron and Hur. We know that Aaron was the brother of Moses, but the Bible doesn't tell us who Hur was, other than that he was from the tribe of Judah. Rabbinic tradition says that Hur was the son of Moses's sister Miriam, and a nephew of Moses and Aaron, but we don't know if that's true.

Moses persevered in prayer, but it took the united effort of two other believers to uphold him in prayer. When Moses lacked the strength to hold his arms high, Aaron and Hur supplied the strength Moses lacked. Do you uphold the arms of your pastors and elders and teachers, or do you try to pull their arms down? I hope you'll see yourself as an Aaron or a Hur.

As long as Moses prayed in his own strength, he grew weary and his hands would fall to his sides. On the battlefield, the Amalekites would gain the advantage. But when Aaron and Hur lifted Moses's arms, Israel gained the advantage.

My friend, you and I can no more stand alone against the flesh, the devil, and the world than a snowflake can survive in a blast furnace. We need to stand together and uphold each other in prayer. That's why it's not enough for Christians to merely go to church every Sunday. As believers, we need to be in small, close-knit groups of Christians who study the Scriptures together, pray for one another, confess their sins and needs to one another, and care for one another. A tightly bonded Christian fellowship is not a luxury. It's an essential part of guarding our souls on the spiritual battlefield.

To win the battle against the flesh, we need to pray the prayer of Moses, the prayer of surrender to God. To win the spiritual battle, we need the support of Aaron and Hur. To win the spiritual battle, we need the courage of Joshua. We cannot win without kneeling in surrender to God, and we cannot win unless we stand together.

The Importance of Waving the Flag

Exodus 17:15 tells us, "Moses built an altar and called it The LORD is my Banner."

As a naturalized citizen of the United States of America, I have often stood to salute the Stars and Stripes—and every time I do, I get goose bumps. Why? Because of all the American flag represents to me. The flag represents the freedom I dreamed of while growing up under a dictatorship in Egypt. The flag reminds me of the men and women who gave their lives for that freedom. It hurts me deeply whenever I see people desecrating the American flag.

After Israel won the victory over the Amalekites, Moses wanted to fly a flag. It was not a flag of freedom. It was a flag of faith. The "flag" of Moses was an altar of sacrifice that bore the Hebrew words *Yahweh Nissi*, "Jehovah is My Banner." Always remember, it is the Lord who gives you victory. It is the Lord who gives you strength. The Lord is your banner.

While walking in London with my eldest grandson, we reached Buckingham Palace. Pointing to the flag over the central facade, I said, "Do you know what that flag means?" It was the Royal Standard of the United Kingdom, representing England, Wales, Scotland, and Northern Ireland. "When you see that flag over Buckingham Palace, it means the Queen is in residence. When you see the Union Flag, it means the Queen is not at the palace."

As I said those words, a thought hit me. When Jesus lives in us, we shouldn't need to tell people, "I'm a Christian." They will know because they will see the Lord's flag over our lives. The banner of the Lord's joy, peace, and love will wave over us.

On October 19, 1968, during the Olympic games in Mexico City, one marathon runner stood out because of the way he ran his race. He was the last-place finisher—yet his story is unforgettable. His name is John Stephen Akhwari from the African nation of Tanzania. During the race, Akhwari suffered muscle cramps and fell to the pavement, dislocating his knee and injuring his shoulder. After being bandaged, Akhwari got up and continued his race.

Most of the spectators had left the stadium by the time Akhwari entered as the last-place finisher. But a few thousand fans cheered him as he limped across the finish line with the bandage flapping from his leg.

After the race, a TV reporter asked why he kept running after his injury. Akhwari replied, "My country did not send me five thousand miles to start the race. They sent me five thousand miles to finish the race."[4]

When your life is emblazoned with the statement "The LORD is my Banner," you may get bloodied in battle, you may suffer wounds and exhaustion. But God is your Banner, and he did not call you to only begin the battle but also to finish it well.

You will persevere. You will prevail. When the battle is over, you will still be standing, waving the flag of the Lord.

▪ QUESTIONS FOR REFLECTION AND DISCUSSION ▪

1. Have you ever tried to win spiritual victories through incomplete obedience? What was the result?

2. In your Christian walk, who is your Moses (whose arms are you upholding)? Who is your Aaron (who uplifts you)? Who is your Joshua (who are you mentoring and sending into battle)?

3. In your Christian walk, do you rely more on prayer or more on action? Do you need to make changes in the way you approach the Christian life?

4. Is your prayer life completely solitary, or do you pray in close fellowship with other believers?

5. After the victory, Moses built an altar called *Yahweh Nissi*, "The LORD is my Banner." Do the people around you know you're a Christian because you live under the Lord's banner? Explain.

12

Tempted to Compromise

Exodus 32

Tennis star Andre Agassi was just nineteen when he signed a contract to appear in a Canon camera commercial. In the ad, he stepped out of a white Lamborghini, tilted his sunglasses down, and said, "Image is everything."

The commercial ran on TV in the summer of 1989—and Agassi soon regretted it. At every tennis match he played, fans shouted, "Image is everything!" When he lost a match, sportscasters wondered aloud if Agassi was all image and no substance. Agassi complained that sportswriters had reduced his entire life to a single slogan, saying, "They predict it's going to be my epitaph."[1]

Agassi eventually lived down the Canon commercial, but the "Image is everything" philosophy lives on. Perhaps the most common example of today's "Image is everything" craze is on social media, where people post glamorized versions of their vacations, their children, and their gourmet meals.

An image is a veneer, a superficial impression, a false front. An image says, "I want popularity, and I'll pay any price to get it." As Christians, we are to reject the "Image is everything" view and instead adopt an "Integrity is everything" philosophy. We should never compromise God's truth or our own integrity to maintain an image. As A. W. Tozer wrote in *Man: The Dwelling Place for God*: "We who preach the gospel must not think of ourselves as public relation agents trying to establish goodwill between God and the world. We must not imagine ourselves commissioned to make Christ acceptable to big business, the press, the world of sports, or even modern education. We are not diplomats but prophets, and our message is not a compromise but an ultimatum."[2]

One of the most tragic examples of spiritual compromise in the Bible is Moses's brother, Aaron. Whenever Aaron was thrust into a position of responsibility, his integrity was found wanting. He was preoccupied with popularity. He would always go along to get along. His motto might well have been "Image is everything."

But before we condemn Aaron and think, *I would never make the compromises he made*, I need to make an honest confession: there is a lot of Aaron in me. And I suspect there may be more of Aaron in you than you realize. Every one of us faces the temptation to compromise. Just one little compromise and you could make that sale, close that deal, or gratify that lust. Every day, we are tempted by the lure of compromise.

Pressure to Compromise

In Exodus 24–31, God takes Moses up on Mount Sinai. There he gives Moses instructions for governing the Israelite people. God also inscribes the Ten Commandments on stone tablets with his finger.

In Exodus 32, the scene shifts to the foot of the mountain. There the people have been waiting impatiently for Moses to return. Finally, the people tell Aaron, "Come, make us gods who will go before us. As for this fellow Moses who brought us up out of Egypt, we don't know what has happened to him" (v. 1).

Aaron goes along with the crowd, saying, "Take off the gold earrings that your wives, your sons and your daughters are wearing, and bring them to me" (v. 2). The people bring their jewelry to Aaron, and he melts it and casts it in the shape of a calf. Then Aaron tells the people, "These are your gods, Israel, who brought you up out of Egypt" (v. 4). Then Aaron builds an altar and announces "a festival to the Lord" the following day. It's a strange mixture of ritual and revelry, with burnt sacrifices, feasting, and drinking.

Meanwhile, on Mount Sinai, God tells Moses, "Go down, because your people, whom you brought up out of Egypt, have become corrupt. They have been quick to turn away from what I commanded them and have made themselves an idol cast in the shape of a calf" (vv. 7–8). God tells Moses he will destroy the Israelites and make a great nation from Moses alone. Moses pleads with God, begging him not to bring disaster on his people. So the Lord relents.

Then Moses goes down the mountain with the two tablets of the law in his hands. He joins Joshua, who had gone partway up the mountain. As they approach the camp of Israel, Joshua hears the noise of the festival and mistakes it for shouts of war, but Moses tells Joshua, "It is not the sound of victory, it is not the sound of defeat; it is the sound of singing that I hear" (v. 18).

Nearing the camp, Moses sees the people dancing in front of the golden calf. In his anger, he throws down the tablets, breaking them in pieces. He punishes the people by grinding the golden calf to dust, scattering the dust on the water, and making the Israelites drink it.

Then Moses says to Aaron, "What did these people do to you, that you led them into such great sin?" (v. 21). Aaron responds by shifting the blame and inventing a lie (more on Aaron's lie in a moment).

Then Moses calls out, "Whoever is for the Lord, come to me" (v. 26). The Levites rally to Moses's side—but many people continue their drunken, idolatrous revelry. So Moses sends the Levites out among the people with swords, and the Levites kill about three thousand rebels.

The next day Moses tells the people, "You have committed a great sin. But now I will go up to the LORD; perhaps I can make atonement for your sin" (v. 30).

Moses again pleads for his people: "Oh, what a great sin these people have committed! They have made themselves gods of gold. But now, please forgive their sin—but if not, then blot me out of the book you have written" (vv. 31–32).

God tells Moses that he will punish their sin at the appropriate time. Exodus 32:35 ends the chapter on this tragic

165

note: "And the LORD struck the people with a plague because of what they did with the calf Aaron had made."

Aaron could have spared his people so much sin and tragedy—but he wanted to be popular. Though he knew that idolatry is an offense against God, Aaron lacked the courage and integrity to stand against the mob. God's truth meant less to Aaron than his own popularity.

Let me share a secret: I feel the pressure to compromise more keenly than you might suppose. Every day, I'm offered the temptation to compromise—and I confess to you, I have considered it. Many times a Christian leader has said to me, "Michael, you preach too much about sin and the blood of Christ—negative subjects from a bygone era" or "Michael, this talk about moral issues is off-putting to today's generation" or "Michael, you need to help people feel good about themselves if you want to be a popular minister."

But God keeps reminding me that I must remain true to the trust he has given me. He reminds me that image is nothing, his truth is everything, and the only audience that matters is that audience of one—Jesus alone.

I'm grateful to be surrounded by friends who ask me about any temptations and challenges in my ministry, who pray for me and hold me accountable, and who encourage me to stay the course. Believe me, I understand the temptation Aaron faced.

Moral and spiritual compromise can ruin a nation, an organization, a church, or a family.

There are three factors that can seduce a seemingly faithful believer to compromise: hunger for approval, relying on clever strategies instead of relying on God, and making excuses instead of accepting responsibility. Let's take a closer look at each of these factors.

Hunger for Approval

There is such a thing as a healthy desire for approval. It's good to be considerate of the feelings of others and to want a good reputation as a Christian. But an unhealthy hunger for approval can seduce us into compromising God's truth. When the desire to be popular and maintain a good image is stronger than our desire for God's approval, then our hunger for approval is unhealthy. As British prime minister Margaret Thatcher said in a 1989 interview, "If you just set out to be liked, you would be prepared to compromise on anything, wouldn't you, at any time? And you would achieve nothing!"[3]

We should want God's approval above all else. We should long to hear him say to us, "Well done, good and faithful servant!" Nowhere do we see Aaron give thought to God's favor. He sought favor only with people. He not only lacked the moral courage to stand against the people, but he was even willing to lead the mutiny against the Lord.

People who hunger for approval are chronically insecure and afraid to rebuke wrongdoing. They avoid making decisions for fear of being criticized. They worry about what others think of them, and they're afraid to express an independent opinion. To them, image is everything.

The apostle Paul gave us God's solution for our approval hunger: "Do not conform to the pattern of this world, but be transformed by the renewing of your mind. Then you will be able to test and approve what God's will is—his good, pleasing and perfect will" (Rom. 12:2).

Reliance on Clever Strategies

There is a powerful lesson in this account that's easily missed: don't rely on your own clever strategies; rely completely on God. We find this principle in Exodus 32:2. After the people come to Aaron demanding he make gods for them, we read, "Aaron answered them, 'Take off the gold earrings that your wives, your sons and your daughters are wearing, and bring them to me.'"

What was Aaron's clever strategy in this verse? He asked the people to surrender their gold. I believe Aaron's plan was to talk the people out of their idolatry and rebellion by placing a high price tag on it. He told them, "Sure, I'll make an idol for you—but it's going to cost you all your gold." Aaron thought the people would say, "Whoa! We didn't know idolatry would hit us in the bank account. Maybe we should reconsider."

Instead of confronting their sin and calling them to repentance, Aaron looked for an easy way out. He tried to appeal to their materialism. Aaron didn't understand that people will give up everything to support their addictions—and idolatry is a deep-seated addiction. We are a materialistic species, but in a contest between materialism and idolatry, false gods always win.

As we saw in chapter 6, the Israelites were attracted to the bull god Apis above all other Egyptian gods. Apis was the Egyptian god of strength. After all the Lord had done for the Israelites, they still wanted to go back to a man-made god of strength. The Israelites had seen God strike down Apis when he struck down the cattle of the Egyptians, yet they still preferred a brutish dead god of metal over the living God who created heaven and earth.

Aaron's strategy backfired when the people willingly paid the price. Aaron outwitted himself. He had to make good on his promise and make the golden calf. The lesson is clear. When you face temptation, don't rely on your own brain power. Don't try to outsmart the devil. Your intellectual resources are no match for Satan. Rely on the wisdom of God alone.

When the golden calf was unveiled, the people said, "These are your gods, Israel, who brought you up out of Egypt" (v. 4). Had the Israelites lost their minds? It was the God of Abraham, Isaac, and Jacob who had brought them out of Egypt—not the bull god Apis. Had the Israelites rejected the Lord in favor of Apis? No, but their intentions were sinful nonetheless.

The Israelites wanted to worship Jehovah in the guise of Apis. They wanted the golden calf to represent Jehovah. They wanted to worship God on their own terms, and they wanted God to conform to their wishes and desires.

The ancient Israelites were no different from so many today, including many who call themselves Christians. They dismiss what God has said about himself in the Bible. They set up an idol of a god in their own minds. "I believe in God," some say, "but I don't believe in a God who punishes sin. I believe in Jesus, but I don't believe he's the only way to God. I believe all religions lead to heaven."

This is twenty-first-century idolatry. There is no difference between making a false mental idol of God today and making a false metal idol in the time of Moses. When God gave the Ten Commandments, he began with these words:

> I am the LORD your God, who brought you out of
> Egypt, out of the land of slavery.

You shall have no other gods before me.
You shall not make for yourself an image in the
    form of anything in heaven above or on the earth
    beneath or in the waters below. (Exod. 20:2–4)

Today, many people who call themselves Christians say that the Bible is wrong in its description of God and that it needs to be edited and revised. They say, for example, "The passages that speak of God judging sexual perversion and other sins need to be understood in their primitive cultural context. After centuries of progress, we've evolved to a point where we know that all forms of sexual behavior are normal. A loving God would never judge people for expressing their sexual identity." These idolatrous ideas are infiltrating many so-called evangelical churches.

As Christians, we don't hate sexually immoral people—we love them with the love of Jesus. We don't condone sin, but neither do we condemn sinners. In John 8, when Jesus dealt with the woman caught in adultery, he dared her accusers, "Let any one of you who is without sin be the first to throw a stone at her" (v. 7). After her accusers had all slunk away, Jesus asked, "Has no one condemned you?" She said, "No one, sir." "Then neither do I condemn you," Jesus said (vv. 10–11).

Many people would like to end the story right there. But Jesus went on to say, "Go now and leave your life of sin" (v. 11). Jesus loves sinners too much to leave them in their sin. And so should we. God is for sinners, but God is against sin—and that should be our mindset. As Christians, we love sinners, but we must never compromise God's truth about sin.

Christians who obey God's Word are increasingly rare in this culture of compromise. Faithfulness to God's truth may

170

earn you persecution on earth, but it will earn rich rewards in heaven. As Jesus said, "Blessed are those who are persecuted because of righteousness, for theirs is the kingdom of heaven" (Matt. 5:10).

Like many compromising Christians, Aaron knew that idolatry is an abomination to God. He knew he should stand for God's truth—but he caved to social pressure. He hungered for approval. With his "clever" scheme, Aaron maneuvered himself into becoming the ringleader of the rebellion against God.

Making Excuses

When Moses confronted Aaron about his role in Israel's sin, Aaron said, "Do not be angry, my lord," and shifted the blame. "You know how prone these people are to evil. They said to me, 'Make us gods who will go before us. As for this fellow Moses who brought us up out of Egypt, we don't know what has happened to him.' So I told them, 'Whoever has any gold jewelry, take it off.' Then they gave me the gold, and I threw it into the fire, and out came this calf!" (Exod. 32:22–24).

God is not fooled. He knows that no one can force us to compromise his truth. Compromise is always a choice, and God will hold us accountable for our choices. There are some who rationalize their sin by saying, "This is just the way God made me. These are the circumstances in which God placed me. He must want me to keep living this way."

Aaron's response to Moses is a classic rationalization: "You know how prone these people are to evil. They said to me, 'Make us gods who will go before us.'" Aaron blamed the people. According to Aaron, they were so persuasive, how could he say no? He couldn't help himself—it was their fault.

Aaron's attempt to pass the buck is as old as Adam and Eve. When God confronted Adam for eating the forbidden fruit, Adam replied, "The woman you put here with me—she gave me some fruit from the tree, and I ate it" (Gen. 3:12). That's a masterpiece of blame shifting. In one sentence, Adam managed to blame both Eve and God: "The woman *you* put here with me . . ."

Then God asked Eve what she had done. She replied, "The serpent deceived me, and I ate" (v. 13). She didn't say, "I made a choice of my own free will." She claimed that the serpent had deceived her. It wasn't her fault—the devil made her do it. But God held Adam and Eve responsible for their disobedient choices, and they lost Paradise.

Aaron must have known that shifting the blame wasn't working. So he tried a different tack, this time making up a bizarre story: "I threw [the gold] into the fire, and out came this calf!" Aaron wanted Moses to believe that when he threw the gold into the fire—poof!—out popped a magical golden calf! Aaron's ridiculous story would be amusing if it weren't so tragic. Aaron was as guilty as sin, and he compounded his guilt with a pitifully absurd lie.

What should Aaron have done? What should any guilty person do when caught red-handed? Confess and repent. But Aaron lacked the character to own up to his sin.

God was prepared to destroy Israel and start over with Moses alone. Only Moses's intercession saved Israel from destruction that day. Not only did Moses plead for mercy for the Israelites, but he was also willing to die in their place.

God did spare Israel—but he did not spare the three thousand people who led the mutiny against God.

We must never take sin and judgment lightly. God may withhold the sentence for sin for a week or a month or even many years, hoping we come to repentance. But if we do not repent, there will be consequences. As Peter reminds us, "The LORD is not slow in keeping his promise, as some understand slowness. Instead he is patient with you, not wanting anyone to perish, but everyone to come to repentance" (2 Pet. 3:9).

Never compromise the gospel of Jesus Christ. Never compromise your integrity. Stand firm for the uncompromised truth of God's Word and you won't be ashamed when you stand in the presence of the Lord.

■ QUESTIONS FOR REFLECTION AND DISCUSSION ■

1. Do you identify with Aaron? Do you struggle with a tendency to compromise, an overeagerness to be accepted or popular?

2. What steps can you take right now to help you stand firm when pressured to compromise?

3. Have you ever tried to achieve righteous or spiritual goals through your own clever human strategy? What was the result? What lessons did you learn?

4. When Moses confronted Aaron about leading Israel into idolatry, Aaron shifted the blame. When you find yourself in a crisis, do you tend to accept responsibility or shift the blame?

5. Do you share the gospel of Jesus Christ with the people around you in an uncompromised, unashamed way? If not, why not? What steps could you take this week to become an uncompromising witness for Christ?

The Envy of Critics

Numbers 12

You're a wife and mother, and you work hard to keep an immaculate house. You have a tender, juicy roast in the oven because your husband's parents are coming for dinner. Everything is perfect. But when your mother-in-law walks in, she looks at you and says, "Dear, you really must do something about your hair!"

You're a husband and father, and you've worked hard to provide your family with a safe and secure home. But your father-in-law always criticizes you: "Don't you know how to fix that leaky faucet?" and "How long has it been since you rotated the tires on your car?"

We all have critics in our lives. They look for our flaws and remind us of our failures. Have you ever wondered why your critics seem to major in minor issues? Often, the minor issue they criticize is not the real reason they're so disapproving. Frequently, your critics attack you out of envy and jealousy. Chronic criticizers elevate themselves by taking others down a notch.

Years ago, a member of our church would criticize every decision I made. He always criticized the most minor matters. He'd say, "I wish you hadn't done that" or "I don't think that was wise." It was a constant source of annoyance, like a pebble in my shoe. His criticism played on my insecurities and caused me to second-guess myself. I wondered, *What if I'm doing it all wrong?*

One day, a thought occurred to me—I believe this insight came from the Lord. I realized that the reason he criticized me over insignificant matters was that his ego was involved. He wanted me to go to him and get his approval over every little matter so that he would feel more important. He wanted to be an unofficial "church boss." For his sake and the sake of the church, I knew I must not yield to his ego. We have elders, committees, a capable staff—in short, a highly effective decision-making team. This man could criticize all he wanted, but it wouldn't change the way the church made decisions.

Once I understood why he was so hypercritical, his words lost their sting. I stopped feeling insecure. From then on, everything he said rolled off like water from a mallard's back.

Chronic criticizers often disguise their criticism: "May I offer a suggestion?" or even "I've been praying for you regarding the decisions you've been making lately." They disguise their criticism to make themselves sound spiritual. If you are not experienced in dealing with such people, you might be manipulated by them.

We will see that Moses had to deal with unfair criticism from a surprising source—his own sister, Miriam, and his brother, Aaron.

When People Criticize You

As a young seminary graduate, I assisted a wise and experienced pastor in California. He taught me many important lessons about serving in the ministry. He said, "When your critics kick you in the rear—rejoice! That means you are out in front, leading."

In Numbers 12, Miriam and Aaron complained about Moses, the man who was out in front, leading. They criticized him for marrying a woman from the kingdom of Cush, the land we now know as Ethiopia. They said to each other, "Has the LORD spoken only through Moses? Hasn't he also spoken through us?" (v. 2).

Verse 3 tells us, "Now Moses was a very humble man, more humble than anyone else on the face of the earth." When God hears Aaron and Miriam criticizing his humble servant Moses, he calls to Moses and his siblings: "Come out to the tent of meeting, all three of you" (v. 4). When they come, God descends in a pillar of cloud to the entrance of the tent, and he tells Aaron and Miriam to step forward. Then the Lord says:

Listen to my words:

When there is a prophet among you,
    I, the LORD, reveal myself to them in visions,
    I speak to them in dreams.

But this is not true of my servant Moses;
    he is faithful in all my house.
With him I speak face to face,
    clearly and not in riddles;
    he sees the form of the LORD.
Why then were you not afraid
    to speak against my servant Moses? (vv. 6–8)

The Lord is angry with Aaron and Miriam, and when the cloud lifts, Miriam's skin is white with leprosy. Aaron pleads with Moses, "I ask you not to hold against us the sin we have so foolishly committed" (v. 11).

Moses cries out in prayer, "Please, God, heal her!" (v. 13).

God agrees to heal Miriam, but she must be sent outside the camp for seven days. So the people of Israel remain in that place until Miriam is permitted to return to the congregation.

What does this story say to us? We see that Miriam and Aaron were envious of their brother Moses and the way God used Moses to lead the people. But instead of honestly expressing the envy and resentment they felt, they focused on a secondary issue: Moses's marriage to a Cushite woman. Instead of honestly confessing, "Moses, we're envious of your leadership position," they criticized him for marrying a foreigner.

I think there is probably a "Miriam" and an "Aaron" in every extended family, in every workplace, and in every church. A Miriam instigates criticism and an Aaron goes along with it. We have already seen that Aaron was a people pleaser who was too cowardly to stand firm for God's truth. He was so wishy-washy we can't tell if Aaron truly agreed with Miriam's criticism of Moses or if he was just being Miriam's yes-man.

And let's be clear about one thing: it isn't gender that makes you a Miriam or an Aaron. There are many men today who are Miriams and many women who are Aarons. What defines a Miriam is an envious, resentful spirit and an eagerness to instigate criticism. What defines an Aaron is a people-pleasing streak that compels them to go along with whatever the criticizer says.

Some of the criticism we receive is justified. Even when criticism is constructive and intended for our good, it hurts to hear it. But unjust, destructive criticism cuts us even more deeply—especially when it comes from someone we love. We feel attacked. We feel betrayed. We feel misunderstood and mistreated.

What makes Miriam and Aaron's criticism so painful for Moses is that they are questioning his character. Miriam is Moses's beloved and trusted sister. It was Miriam who had watched over baby Moses and saved his life when he floated helplessly in a basket at the edge of the Nile. When Moses grew to become a man, Miriam and Aaron saw him turn his back on the gold of Egypt and identify with the sufferings of the Israelites. But now Moses's own nearest and dearest ones, his sister and brother, falsely accuse him of selfish motives.

Here is what I have learned about critical people: those who are the most eager to offer criticism are usually the least willing to receive constructive criticism. They have the thinnest of skins. They can dish it out, but they can't take it.

Critical people never feel good about themselves. They have never learned to be content where God has placed them, so they strike out at others and try to bring people down.

They lash out at people they think are more important than they are, more successful than they are, or more popular than they are. If you never want to be criticized, simply say nothing, attempt nothing, and accomplish nothing. Chronic criticizers will leave you alone because you'll have done nothing for them to envy. But if you achieve anything notable, if you do good works that bless other people, count on this: they will attack you.

Today, we regard George Washington as America's first (and perhaps greatest) president. But in his own day, Washington was frequently subjected to unjust criticism. John Beckley, clerk of the House of Representatives, wrote an anonymous opinion piece, saying that "the mask of political hypocrisy has been alike worn by a Caesar, a Cromwell and a Washington." And Thomas Paine, who helped ignite the American revolution with his pamphlet *Common Sense*, wrote during Washington's second term: "It is laughable to hear Mr. Washington talk of his sympathetic feelings, who has always been remarked, even among his friends, for not having any. . . . [Washington's character] is a sort of nondescribable, chameleon-colored thing."[1]

Another great president, Abraham Lincoln, suffered even more libelous criticism in his own time. As he was traveling by train to Washington for his first inauguration, Lincoln's home-state newspaper, the *Salem Advocate* of central Illinois, published a scathing editorial. The newspaper said that Lincoln's "weak, wishy-washy, namby-pamby efforts, imbecile in matter, disgusting in manner, have made us the laughingstock of the whole world. The European powers will despise us because we have no better material out of which to make a President."[2]

Historian Donald Phillips observed, "Abraham Lincoln was slandered, libeled, and hated perhaps more intensely than any other man to ever run for the nation's highest office. . . . Lincoln was publicly called just about every name imaginable by the press of the day, including grotesque baboon, a third-rate country lawyer who once split rails and now splits the Union, a coarse vulgar joker, a dictator, an ape, a buffoon, and others."[3]

The next time someone unfairly criticizes you, remember that you are in good company—Moses, Washington, and Lincoln. The people who receive the most unfair criticism are usually those who are busy accomplishing great things and serving people. When attacked, take comfort in this truth.

Comparing and Criticizing

What sort of wrongdoing did Miriam and Aaron accuse Moses of? Simply this: Moses took a wife who was not "one of us." He married a woman from Cush.

Years earlier, Moses had married another foreign-born woman, Zipporah, a Midianite. He married her after fleeing Egypt but before receiving God's call at the burning bush. There's no hint in the Bible that Miriam and Aaron ever criticized Moses for his first marriage, even though the circumstances were similar.

Why did Miriam and Aaron criticize Moses over his second marriage? From a New Testament perspective, we understand the principle Paul set forth in 2 Corinthians 6:14: "Do not be yoked together with unbelievers. For what do righteousness and wickedness have in common? Or what fellowship can light have with darkness?" Of course, Paul wrote those words centuries after Moses lived. In fact, the Scriptures didn't exist until God inspired Moses to write the first books of the Bible. Also, the fact that Moses's wives were foreign born does not necessarily mean they were unbelievers. Because of Moses's influence, they probably converted to faith in the God of Abraham, Isaac, and Jacob.

So what logic do Miriam and Aaron offer for criticizing their brother? None! There is no logic behind their criticism because criticism motivated by envy is not logical.

Miriam, Aaron, and Moses all had the same father and mother. They were flesh-and-blood siblings. They too were chosen by God to play a role in the deliverance of God's people. Miriam was a song leader and choir director. Aaron was a high priest.

But it was Moses who was called by God at the burning bush. It was Moses who was chosen by God to be the deliverer and lawgiver of Israel. It was only by the grace of God that Miriam and Aaron were born into the same family as Moses. They had no reason to feel slighted or discontented because God had called Moses. They should have felt nothing but gratitude.

The Bible does not explain Miriam's irrational criticism. Some Jewish commentators have tried to make sense of it, speculating that perhaps Moses's first wife had died, and Moses had married a woman from Cush without getting Miriam's advice and blessing. We don't know if that's true, but this explanation is consistent with human nature.

Some chronic criticizers don't want you to make a move without their approval. Their ego is involved. It's a point of pride that you seek out their opinion. If you don't consult with them, their feelings are hurt, their pride is wounded, and they will criticize you without mercy. Will they criticize you for not consulting with them? No, because they know that the real reason would sound selfish and petty, so they pick some other reason to rake you over the coals. They criticize you because of the person you married or because of something your children did or for some other absurd reason. But they are punishing you for not stroking their egos.

We don't know if that was Miriam's motivation for criticizing Moses. It's a plausible speculation, but most Christian scholars hold a different view. According to this view, Moses was separated from his first wife, Zipporah, and his children and father-in-law, Jethro, when he went to Egypt and confronted Pharaoh. During that separation, what family did Moses have? Only Miriam and Aaron. During that time, Miriam had prestige as the sister of Moses. She was the queen bee in Israel—until this Cushite woman stole the show. Miriam felt upstaged by the new Mrs. Moses. With the help of weak-willed Aaron, Miriam tried to take Moses down a peg. Chronic criticizers always build themselves up by taking others down.

If I criticize you, it's because I think I'm superior to you— morally superior, spiritually superior, or intellectually superior. Chronic criticizers are always comparing themselves to other people: "Compared to that guy, I'm a pretty good Christian. I'm wiser, more moral, and more spiritual." But God doesn't compare us with other people. He measures our lives according to an absolute standard of morality, spirituality, and reliance on God. We have no right to criticize another servant of God.

God does not always call those who are the most brilliant, the cleverest, the most talented, or the best educated. He is often pleased to use the least brilliant and least talented people to achieve his eternal plan. As Paul writes, "But God chose the foolish things of the world to shame the wise; God chose the weak things of the world to shame the strong. God chose the lowly things of this world and the despised things—and the things that are not—to nullify the things that are" (1 Cor. 1:27–28). Let's not be quick to judge and criticize those whom God chooses and uses for his glory.

Pray for Your Chronic Criticizer

There's an old saying in the Middle East: "If one man calls you a donkey, ignore him. But if ten men call you a donkey, go buy a saddle." Moses had two critics—he wasn't ready to be fitted for a saddle.

The criticism against Moses was unfair and libelous—and blatantly sinful. Moses could have lashed out—but he didn't. He could have accused his siblings of hypocrisy—but he didn't. He could have defended his decision to marry a woman from Cush—but he didn't. Sometimes it's appropriate to defend ourselves, as Jesus defended himself against the accusations of the Pharisees. But Moses didn't need to defend himself.

Moses didn't seem troubled by the criticism of Miriam and Aaron. He knew that if his brother and sister were truly concerned about his marriage, they would have spoken to him privately. Moses probably understood that Miriam had some ego issues. He knew that his siblings were stewing

184

in their own envy. He may have felt more pity than anger toward them, and that may explain his forgiving spirit toward Miriam and Aaron.

Because of his humility and his love for his sister and brother, Moses didn't need to lash out at them. Because God was his defender, Moses didn't need to defend himself. Moses recalled how Miriam had watched over him and saved his life when he was a baby. Moses knew that, despite Miriam's character flaws, she had a genuine heart for God. She displayed her love for God in a song of praise she composed after Israel was delivered from the Red Sea. Aaron, despite his weaknesses, had stood at Moses's side throughout the confrontation with Pharaoh.

We should remember this principle whenever we are unfairly criticized: between the slanderer and the slandered, there is God; between the attacker and the victim, there is God. When Miriam and Aaron attacked Moses, God intervened.

Miriam was stricken with leprosy. You may wonder why God punished Miriam but not Aaron. But I believe Aaron was punished as well. As the high priest, it was his agonizing duty to pronounce his sister, Miriam, unclean.

How did Moses respond to God's judgment against Miriam and Aaron? He responded with impassioned prayer. Numbers 12:13 tells us, "So Moses cried out to the LORD, 'Please, God, heal her!'" When the Bible tells us that Moses "cried out," we should recognize the anguished emotions behind those two words.

Praying for those who hurt us is one of the most healing experiences of the Christian life. Moses prayed for his sister to be healed—and that prayer healed Moses as well. When you ask God to bless your enemy, there's no room in your heart for hatred.

Moses prayed for Miriam, and God answered his prayer. God healed Miriam after seven days. Why seven days? Why didn't he heal Miriam instantly? I believe God wanted to teach the people of Israel an important moral lesson: sin can be forgiven, but sin still has lingering consequences. Miriam had to learn that, and so did the people of Israel.

Those who habitually criticize a spouse, child, employee, friend, pastor, or fellow Christian often do so without realizing it. It's so chronic they don't even realize the harm they cause. Ask God to make you aware when you criticize the people in your life. Ask him to give you a more tolerant, understanding spirit. Ask the Holy Spirit to fill you and empower you to bless others and build them up instead of tearing them down.

Are you a target of unjust criticism? Ask God to replace bitterness with forgiveness. Ask him to empower you to pray for those who criticize and slander you. It's not easy, especially when the wounds are fresh. But if you persevere in prayer, and follow the example of Moses, you'll find that praying for your critics will grow easier day by day.

■ **QUESTIONS FOR REFLECTION AND DISCUSSION** ■

1. Are you a "Miriam" who instigates criticism? Are you an "Aaron" who hesitates to stand for the truth? What can you do to overcome this tendency?

2. Can you recall a time when you were criticized for doing good works? How did you respond? What did you learn?

3. Chronic criticizers think they are morally, spiritually, or intellectually superior to those they criticize. Do you struggle with a superior attitude? What can you do to overcome this tendency?

4. Someone once said, "Comparison is the thief of joy." Have you found that comparing yourself with others steals your joy and robs you of contentment?

5. Are you the target of unfair criticism? Can you forgive and pray for the chronic criticizers in your life? Why or why not?

Lord of the Impossible

Numbers 13–14

In the early 1980s, I studied human institutions at Emory University. I learned that institutions are social structures that govern the behavior of individuals and communities. I learned about different kinds of human institutions, such as families, peer groups, language groups, legal systems, governments, and so forth. Even a visible, local church is a human institution.

Though there are many kinds of human institutions, there is only one divine institution, founded and sustained by God himself: the church universal, consisting of elect believers from every nation and every generation. Unlike a local church body or a denomination, the divine institution is an invisible institution. It has no earthly human leader, no board of directors, no organizational structure.

In my studies, I found that human institutions—including churches—are generally made up of three kinds of people: the top 10 percent, the middle 80 percent, and the bottom 10 percent. The top 10 percent are visionaries—people who envision the future. They are eager to turn possibilities into realities. Some are visionary leaders who say, "Who's with me? Follow me into the future!" Others are visionary followers who say, "Lead on! I believe in your vision! I'm with you!" Whether leaders or followers, visionaries embrace change and make change happen.

The next group, the middle 80 percent, is the undecided majority. They are like the good people of Missouri, the "Show Me State." The majority in any human institution will get behind a vision, but only if you convince them the vision is good for them. "Prove it to me," they say, "then I'll get behind it."

Finally, there is the bottom 10 percent—the unpersuadables. They are the ones who sing, "We shall not be moved!" Their feet are sunk in cement. They disagree with everything. You say "up," they say "down." You say, "Let's go," they say, "Whoa!"

In my experience, these 10-80-10 proportions are fairly consistent in every institution. Envisioning the future isn't easy, even for the forward-thinking 10 percent. Human history is filled with examples of brilliant, far-seeing people who made confident but shortsighted pronouncements about the future. Following are some examples.

On May 1, 1486, Italian explorer Christopher Columbus approached Queen Isabella of Spain with a plan to discover new lands by sailing west. The queen assembled a committee of advisors to study Columbus's proposal. The committee reported, "So many centuries after the Creation, it is unlikely that anyone could find hitherto unknown lands of any value."

In 1774, after the Boston Tea Party demonstrated growing unrest among American colonists, the British prime minister Lord North confidently declared that any revolution could be quickly put down, saying, "Four or five frigates will do the business without any military force."

In 1825, the *Quarterly Review* ridiculed the notion that railroads would ever carry passengers at speeds of ten miles an hour or more. "What can be more palpably absurd," the editors wrote, "than the prospect held out of locomotives travelling twice as fast as stagecoaches?"[1]

Most of the progress we now take for granted was once considered impossible. This principle applies in the spiritual realm as well.

Where we see impossibilities, God sees opportunities. Where we see roadblocks, God sees pathways. In Numbers 13–14, God calls Israel to go forward and possess the promised land. But the people pull back in fear, declaring God's command "impossible." In these two Old Testament chapters, we find a profoundly important lesson: our God is Lord of the impossible.

The Majority and the Minority

After traveling for more than a year since leaving Egypt, the Israelites reached the border of the promised land. They could have taken a much shorter route, but God led them the long way around. Why? He wanted to teach them to trust him, to lean on him, to obey him.

In Numbers 13, Israel is camped at Kadesh in the desert. God tells Moses to send spies into Canaan, one spy from each tribe: "Send some men to explore the land of Canaan, which I am giving to the Israelites" (v. 2). God did not say, "the land I hope to give to the Israelites." He said, "the land of Canaan, which I am giving to the Israelites."

Two names stand out among the twelve—Caleb from the tribe of Judah and Hoshea (whom Moses renamed Joshua) from the tribe of Ephraim. Moses sent them up through the Negev Desert and into the hill country to inspect the land, the orchards, the vineyards, the fortifications, and the inhabitants.

When the spies returned forty days later, they brought back some of the fruit of the land—pomegranates, figs, and a huge cluster of grapes. And I mean huge. That cluster of grapes was so big and heavy it took two men to carry it on a pole between them. (A stylized image of that cluster of grapes, suspended between two walking men, is the official logo of Israel's Ministry of Tourism today.)

The majority reported, "We went into the land to which you sent us, and it does flow with milk and honey! Here is its fruit. But the people who live there are powerful, and the cities are fortified and very large. . . . We can't attack those people; they are stronger than we are" (vv. 27–28, 31).

Then Caleb stood and gave the minority report: "We should go up and take possession of the land, for we can certainly do it" (v. 30).

The fearmongering majority argued, "The land we explored devours those living in it. All the people we saw there are of great size. We saw the Nephilim there (the descendants of Anak come from the Nephilim). We seemed like grasshoppers in our own eyes" (vv. 32–33).

Both sides agreed on one thing: the promised land was as rich and bountiful as the Lord had promised. The ten spies of the majority and the two spies of the minority only disagreed about what they should do about it. The majority disregarded God's vision for Israel and substituted human analysis. They left God out of the equation and declared the conquest of Canaan impossible. The minority—Joshua and Caleb—took God at his word.

Numbers 14 tells of the rebellious response of the people. The Israelites wept and grumbled against Moses and Aaron. "If only we had died in Egypt! Or in this wilderness! Why is the LORD bringing us to this land only to let us fall by the sword? Our wives and children will be taken as plunder. Wouldn't it be better for us to go back to Egypt?" (vv. 2–3). Many wanted to replace Moses with a new leader who would lead them back to slavery in Egypt.

This rebellion provoked an anguished response from the faithful minority. Moses and Aaron fell facedown in front of the assembly, and Joshua and Caleb tore their clothes, saying, "The land we passed through and explored is exceedingly good. If the LORD is pleased with us, he will lead us into that land, a land flowing with milk and honey, and will give it to us. Only do not rebel against the LORD" (vv. 7–9).

But the people talked about stoning Moses, Aaron, Joshua, and Caleb to death.

Then God spoke to Moses from the cloud of glory at the meeting tent: "How long will these people treat me with contempt? How long will they refuse to believe in me, in spite of all the signs I have performed among them? I will strike them down with a plague and destroy them, but I will make you into a nation greater and stronger than they" (vv. 11–12).

Moses again pleaded with God to show mercy:

If you put all these people to death, leaving none alive,
the nations who have heard this report about you will say,
"The LORD was not able to bring these people into the land
he promised them on oath, so he slaughtered them in the
wilderness."
  Now may the Lord's strength be displayed, just as you have
declared: "The LORD is slow to anger, abounding in love and
forgiving sin and rebellion. . . . In accordance with your great
love, forgive the sin of these people, just as you have pardoned
them from the time they left Egypt until now." (vv. 15–19)

The Lord answered, "I have forgiven them, as you asked.
Nevertheless, as surely as I live and as surely as the glory of
the LORD fills the whole earth, not one of those who saw my
glory and the signs I performed in Egypt and in the wilderness but who disobeyed me and tested me ten times—not
one of them will ever see the land I promised on oath to their
ancestors. No one who has treated me with contempt will
ever see it" (vv. 20–23).

God promised Joshua and Caleb that he would allow them
to inherit the land because they trusted the Lord. All the
other Israelites would wander in the wilderness for forty
years—one year for each day the spies explored the land—as
punishment for their unfaithfulness.

Trusting God for the Impossible

Four principles emerge from Numbers 13–14: (1) The majority is always wrong—unless! (2) Obedience, not opinion,

always brings God's blessing. (3) Obedient faith turns giants into grasshoppers. (4) God always rewards obedience. Let's look at each of these four principles in turn.

The Majority Is Always Wrong—Unless!

The first principle that emerges from this account is that the majority is always wrong—unless the majority is centered on God. There was a time when most Americans believed in God, feared God, and honored God. That's why God so richly blessed America in times past. As the psalmist writes:

> Blessed is the nation whose God is the LORD,
> the people he chose for his inheritance. (Ps. 33:12)

But in Numbers 13, ten of the twelve spies returned and said, "We can't attack those people; they are stronger than we are." The ten spies looked at the obstacles in the promised land and saw only impossibilities. As soon as the majority gave their report, the people gave in to despair.

What was at stake? God's character. God's promises. God's own word. The ten spies of the majority looked at the promised land from a human perspective—and were filled with fear. The two spies of the minority saw the promised land from God's perspective—and were filled with confidence.

It's said there is safety in numbers, but that's not true in the spiritual realm. Safety is found only in the center of God's will. If you are out of God's will, then you're wrong even when you are in the majority. If you're in God's will, you're safe and secure even as a minority of one.

Opinion versus Obedience

The second principle that emerges from this account is that only obedience—not opinion—brings about God's blessings.

God had promised the land to Abraham four hundred years earlier. He had reaffirmed that promise to Moses. God confirmed his promise through supernatural interventions and by delivering Israel from slavery in Egypt. He gave the people his Holy Spirit to lead them as a cloud of glory. He gave them food from heaven to sustain them on the way to the promised land. I Ie supernaturally kept their clothes and sandals from wearing out.

Finally, God told them it was time to go into the promised land to possess it. It was time for obedience. What did the people do? They listened to the opinion of ten of the twelve spies—and refused to obey God.

Here is the 80 percent principle at work in Israel. Most of the Israelites said, in effect, "God, we need proof that you won't let us down. Those Canaanites are huge and mean, and they could stomp on us as if we were grasshoppers! We choose the majority opinion over obedience."

Friend in Christ, you have experienced the joy of salvation. You can point to many times God has intervened and blessed you unexpectedly. Then, after receiving so much from God's hand, you encounter a roadblock, a daunting challenge. How do you respond? Do you side with the majority and turn back? Or do you keep moving forward?

Do you choose opinion—or obedience?

Sometimes our circumstances drive us to the most unbiblical opinions: "God must not love me anymore!" "God has abandoned me!" "God has forgotten me!" That was the majority opinion among the Israelites, despite the miraculous proofs of God's love for them.

During the early years of The Church of The Apostles, our small but growing congregation met in a public school. We tried to purchase property but ran into one obstacle after another. I heard some of the most outlandish opinions from some: "We must not be in the will of God—if we were, we would have found a place by now." "Maybe God doesn't want us to start this church." "Maybe God wants us to disband."

I admit these opinions sometimes sounded persuasive. Psychologists have long known of a phenomenon called "herd mentality" or "groupthink." When enough people express the same opinion again and again, individuals feel pressured to conform. I had moments when I felt I should walk away—but deep down, I knew better. I had heard God clearly when he gave me the vision to plant a church to impact the globe. I knew it was obedience, not opinion, that mattered to God. He would bless our obedience but not our opinions.

The fleshly temptation to conform to opinions is why the apostle Paul wrote, "Do not conform to the pattern of this world, but be transformed by the renewing of your mind. Then you will be able to test and approve what God's will is—his good, pleasing and perfect will" (Rom. 12:2).

In our walk with Christ, we will face obstacles. In our walk with Christ, we will encounter giants and seemingly impossible situations. In our walk with Christ, we will hear many differing opinions—and we'll be tempted to doubt God. If you yield to the temptation to conform to majority opinion, you'll stop daring great things for God. You'll miss the blessings that come with obeying God's good and perfect will.

So I challenge you: don't be distracted, don't be deterred by the opinions of the majority, obey the will of the Lord—then prepare to be amazed at all the unexpected ways he works through your life. The people around you will no longer squeeze you into their mold by their opinions. Instead, you'll influence them for Christ through your obedience.

Dare to believe the Word of God. Dare to obey him unconditionally. Dare to say to the giants in your life: "You are nothing but grasshoppers in the sight of our awesome God."

Turning Giants into Grasshoppers

The third principle that emerges from this account is that giants can become grasshoppers when we view them with eyes of faith. When the twelve spies returned, ten saw the Canaanites as giants and themselves as grasshoppers. Two, Joshua and Caleb, saw the inhabitants as grasshoppers and themselves as giants. Why? Because Joshua and Caleb had eyes of faith.

Numbers 13:30 tells us, "Then Caleb silenced the people before Moses and said, 'We should go up and take possession of the land, for we can certainly do it.'" I love the take-charge faith Caleb demonstrated. He didn't doubt God for a moment.

Over the years, I've known a number of "Calebs." They fire everybody up to accomplish great things. They are warriors of faith, champions of obedience. It's not easy to be a Caleb. A true Caleb dares to challenge the wrath of the angry, unbelieving mob. You cannot be a Caleb without making enemies.

Negative, critical people hate Calebs. Why? Because they envy people of faith. Negative people like to think of themselves as realists, and they think of Calebs as impractical, idealistic dreamers. But the so-called realism of the negative thinkers is nothing but faithlessness. Like the ten faithless spies and most of the Israelite people, they declare obedience to God "impossible."

Joshua and Caleb pleaded, "Do not rebel against the LORD. And do not be afraid of the people of the land, because we will devour them. Their protection is gone, but the LORD is with us. Do not be afraid of them" (Num. 14:9).

When you speak as Joshua and Caleb spoke, expect criticism. Expect enemies to rise up against you, as they rose up against Joshua and Caleb. The whole assembly of Israel talked about stoning Moses, Aaron, Joshua, and Caleb. If the Lord had not surrounded them with his protective hand, those four men of faith might have ended up under a pile of stones.

Has God called you to an "impossible" challenge? Are there giants in the land? Do you feel like a grasshopper under the gaze of your enemies? God turns giants into grasshoppers for those who believe in him.

The Rewards of Obedience

The fourth principle that emerges from this account is that God rewards obedience. We may not experience that reward according to our timetable, but God always keeps his word.

In Joshua 14, forty-five years after the events in Numbers 14, we read that Joshua and Caleb have entered the promised land. The army of Israel has conquered the land. Now it's time for Caleb to receive the allotment of land Moses promised him. Caleb says to Joshua:

> You know what the Lord said to Moses the man of God at Kadesh Barnea about you and me. I was forty years old when Moses the servant of the Lord sent me from Kadesh Barnea to explore the land. And I brought him back a report according to my convictions, but my fellow Israelites who went up with me made the hearts of the people melt in fear. I, however, followed the Lord my God wholeheartedly. So on that day Moses swore to me, "The land on which your feet have walked will be your inheritance and that of your children forever, because you have followed the Lord my God wholeheartedly."
>
> Now then, just as the Lord promised, he has kept me alive for forty-five years since the time he said this to Moses, while Israel moved about in the wilderness. So here I am today, eighty-five years old! I am still as strong today as the day Moses sent me out; I'm just as vigorous to go out to battle now as I was then. Now give me this hill country that the Lord promised me that day. You yourself heard then that the Anakites were there and their cities were large and fortified, but, the Lord helping me, I will drive them out just as he said. (vv. 6–12)

So Joshua gave Caleb the hill country known as Hebron. "Then," Scripture tells us, "the land had rest from war" (v. 15). What confidence Caleb had! He believed that the bigger God's enemies, the harder they fall. Caleb knew God was in the giant-killing business.

Caleb's faith undoubtedly inspired a young shepherd boy (and future king) named David to face a Philistine giant armed only with a sling and five stones. That shepherd boy had a Caleb-like faith in God, and he faced his giant with confidence.

God has not changed. The principles of faith and obedience have not changed. What was true for Joshua and Caleb and David is still true today. We see crises and impossibilities in our families, our churches, and our nation. We read news of global pandemics, economic crises, political crises, and moral crises—but these are merely symptoms of the real crisis of our time—a crisis of unbelief and disobedience. The solution is to commit to faith in the Word of God.

Today, so-called Christian pastors, authors, and leaders are declaring that the Bible doesn't mean what it says and that Jesus is not the way, the truth, and the life. False teachers have infiltrated evangelical churches. Christian publishers are distributing books that deny the validity of Scripture and dismiss the atoning death and resurrection of Christ.

Could this be the great falling away Paul predicted in 2 Thessalonians 2? Could we be entering the time Jesus spoke of when he said, "At that time many will turn away from the faith and will betray and hate each other, and many false prophets will appear and deceive many people" (Matt. 24:10–11)? I don't know—but I do know this: when Jesus returns, I want to be found in the camp of Joshua and Caleb, not the camp of the unfaithful 80 percent.

Caleb's faith was like a fountain of youth. At age eighty-five, he said, "I am still as strong today as the day Moses sent me out; I'm just as vigorous to go out to battle now as I was then." How did Caleb's faith keep him youthful? I believe it's because Caleb never worried. No matter what crises arose in his life, he trusted God. That's called "resting in the Lord."

During the forty years Israel wandered in the wilderness, most of the Israelites felt their strength ebbing away as they aged. But Caleb seemed to grow younger and stronger. He was renewed daily by his confidence in the Lord.

Caleb's faith turned giants into grasshoppers. If the people of Israel had listened to Joshua and Caleb, how different their lives would have been. They would have marched into the land and possessed it by faith. They would have said, "Boo!" to the giants of Canaan, and those giants would have fled in terror.

Don't believe the opinion of the majority. Believe God. Obey God. Then go out and slay giants in his name.

■ QUESTIONS FOR REFLECTION AND DISCUSSION ■

1. In your church and your Christian life, are you in the top 10 percent (visionaries), the middle 80 percent (the "prove it to me" group), or the bottom 10 percent ("we shall not be moved")? If you are in the top 10 percent, are you a visionary leader or a visionary follower?

2. What is the great "impossible" challenge you face right now? Sacrificial giving? Sharing your faith? Risking to serve God and others? What can you do to increase your faith and obedience?

3. When you make decisions, are you primarily guided by the opinions of others or by God's Word?

4. Have you ever been so convinced of the rightness of your position that you were willing to stand against the majority? Have you ever voted with the majority because you lacked the courage to stand alone? What did you learn from those experiences?

Wrongful Wrath

Numbers 20:1–13

One Sunday morning many years ago, I sat in a church listening to a false teacher deliver a sermon that was completely heretical. He denied the authority of God's Word and claimed that all religions lead to God. Hearing falsehood from a church pulpit filled me with a righteous anger. That anger was the catalyst that led to the founding of The Church of The Apostles.

Anger is a natural emotion. Everyone gets angry from time to time. The gospel accounts make it clear that Jesus became angry on several occasions—yet even in his anger, he did not sin. Anger can be a destructive force—or an enormously constructive force. It depends on how we manage our anger.

When anger is mishandled, it can destroy relationships, end marriages, divide churches, ruin reputations, and worse.

Uncontrolled anger has shattered hopes and dreams. Unresolved anger has blocked many blessings and answers to prayer. Anger that turns into bitterness can endanger one's physical and mental health.

Much of the anger we experience begins with frustration. We easily become frustrated when we are stuck in traffic, when the plumbing backs up, or when our spouse fails to appreciate our Solomon-like wisdom. We are tempted to lash out, either verbally (with insults, swearing, or threats) or physically (slamming a fist on the table or punching a wall).

Many people make excuses for their anger: "I have a short fuse—that's just the way I am" or "I inherited my quick temper from my parents." These are all flimsy excuses for not placing our emotions under the control of the Holy Spirit.

With Moses in the School of Sanctification

I vividly recall a day in 1973 when I went on my face before the Lord and begged him to either change me or revoke my calling to the ministry. I had a quick temper, and sometimes my anger led me to do and say things I was later ashamed of. I could not see how someone as quick-tempered as I was could be God's servant.

Some of my friends talked about "deliverance" from bad habits and undesirable character traits. The way they described it, God would somehow zap you and alter your character. You could be instantly delivered, they said, from addiction, lust, gluttony, and, yes, anger. I loved that idea, and I prayed fervently for God to deliver me from my quick temper.

Alas, I did not experience an instantaneous deliverance. In time, I realized God was speaking to me through the still, small voice of the Holy Spirit. He was saying, "I will answer your prayer, Michael, but I will not zap you. There's no quick fix. You must go through my School of Sanctification."

Sanctification—becoming set apart for God's use—is a process of learning and growing. And here's breaking news: I still have not graduated from God's School of Sanctification. God is still hammering and chiseling at my character and gradually conforming me to the image of Christ. When will God finish the job of molding and shaping my character? The day you hear that Michael Youssef has departed this life and entered into glory, that's the day I'll receive my diploma from God's School of Sanctification.

One reason I haven't graduated yet is that I keep flunking the required courses, one of which is Godly Anger Management. God continues to tutor me and take me to higher and higher levels of study.

In Numbers 20, we find Moses studying at the School of Sanctification, and we see God teaching him an important life lesson. Previously, in Numbers 13–14, we saw Moses displaying godly character by expressing forgiveness to his sister, Miriam, and his brother, Aaron. Moses prayed for those who slandered him, and God answered his prayer. But here in Numbers 20, we find Moses at a spiritual low point.

I'm grateful that God is the author of the Bible. The Spirit inspired human writers to set down stories of people such as Abraham, Isaac, Jacob, Moses, King David, King Solomon, Queen Esther, and the rest. The Spirit didn't edit out their flaws and foibles. He didn't bleach out their sins and failings.

The Bible shows us the human condition with unflinching candor.

Why didn't God show us only the faithfulness, strength, and courage of Moses? Why did God also show us Moses's failings and weaknesses? God's Word presents an accurate, unretouched picture of the heroes of the Bible so that we will be able to identify with them and be encouraged by them. Whatever challenges they overcame, we can overcome as well. We have weaknesses—so did they. We falter and fail—so did they.

Moses didn't receive his sanctification diploma during his lifetime, and neither will we. Moses had a spiritual Achilles' heel—a quick and unruly temper. And his anger would ultimately cost him dearly: God would deny Moses entrance into the promised land.

This sad chapter in the life of Moses should motivate each of us to pray that God would equip us to persevere in our sanctification, to learn self-control and godliness in every area in which we are tempted. For Moses, the flaw in his character was anger. You might struggle with a different flaw—pride, greed, laziness, lust, gluttony, or envy. But we all struggle, and we are all students in God's School of Sanctification.

Frustration and Exasperation

As Numbers 20 opens, we find that Israel has again camped at Kadesh in the desert, the place from which Israel had sent the twelve spies into the promised land nearly four decades earlier. There Miriam died and was buried.

The people had no water, and they blamed Moses and Aaron, saying (and by now, this is a familiar refrain): "If only we had died when our brothers fell dead before the LORD! Why did you bring the LORD's community into this wilderness, that we and our livestock should die here? Why did you bring us up out of Egypt to this terrible place? It has no grain or figs, grapevines or pomegranates. And there is no water to drink!" (vv. 3–5).

These faithless people have only themselves to blame. If they had obeyed God and trusted the report of Joshua and Caleb, they would be enjoying grain, figs, grapes, and pomegranates in the land of milk and honey. Instead, they are thirsting in the desert and complaining against Moses and the Lord.

Moses and Aaron went to the entrance of the tent of meeting, and the glory of the Lord appeared to them. God said, "Take the staff, and you and your brother Aaron gather the assembly together. Speak to that rock before their eyes and it will pour out its water" (v. 8).

So Moses gathered the people in front of the rock and shouted, "Listen, you rebels, must we bring you water out of this rock?" (v. 10). Then he struck the rock twice with his staff and water gushed forth. The people and their livestock had plenty to drink.

But God hadn't told Moses to strike the rock. God had said, "Speak to that rock." So God said to Moses and Aaron, "Because you did not trust in me enough to honor me as holy in the sight of the Israelites, you will not bring this community into the land I give them" (v. 12). The spring of water that God provided became known as Meribah, which means "quarreling," because the Israelites had quarreled with God.

For nearly four decades, Moses had led the Israelites in the wilderness, enduring their constant complaining. Finally, Moses lost patience with the people. In his frustration, he exceeded God's command to speak to the rock. He allowed his anger to control him and lead him into disobedience.

Righteous and Unrighteous Anger

On one level, the anger of Moses is understandable. How much bickering can one man stand? But this is not the first time Moses allowed anger to control his actions. In this account, Moses is 120 years old. Looking back over the life of Moses, we see his anger management issues go back to his early years.

In Exodus 2, Moses lost control when he saw an Egyptian slave driver beating an Israelite slave. Moses had full authority as the adopted son of the Pharaoh to take the Egyptian aside and order him to treat the Israelite with respect. Instead, the anger of Moses boiled over and drove him to commit murder. The Bible tells us Moses looked to the right and to the left, and when he saw no one watching, he killed the Egyptian and buried the body.

Moses graduated summa cum laude from Heliopolis University—proof that education alone does not civilize a man. Only the life-changing power of the cross of Jesus and the indwelling power of the Holy Spirit can civilize us and enable us to master our primitive impulses. Learning self-control takes a lifetime and requires us to cooperate with God as he teaches us, sanctifies us, and reshapes our character.

Later, as Moses sought to deliver the Israelites from slavery, he again allowed his anger to control him. In Exodus 11, Moses went before Pharaoh to warn him of the tenth judgment, the death of the firstborn sons. Moses warned, "There will be loud wailing throughout Egypt—worse than there has ever been or ever will be again" (v. 6). Verse 8 tells us that, after delivering God's warning to Pharaoh, "Moses, hot with anger, left Pharaoh."

Moses knew that God was giving Pharaoh exactly what he wanted—a hard heart, a stony and immovable will. Even so, Moses was consumed with rage over Pharaoh's stubbornness. Frederick Buechner explains how Moses might have felt as he seethed in rage toward Pharaoh:

> Of the seven deadly sins, anger is possibly the most fun. To lick your wounds, to smack your lips over the grievances long past, to roll over your tongue the prospect of bitter confrontations still to come, to savor to the last toothsome morsel both the pain you are given and the pain you are giving back—in many ways it is a feast fit for a king. The chief drawback is that what you are wolfing down is yourself. The skeleton at the feast is you.[1]

Another time Moses let his anger control him was when he came down from the mountain with the stone tablets in his hands. It was the most precious document ever given to the human race, the Ten Commandments, inscribed by the finger of God. When Moses found the people of Israel carousing and worshiping the Egyptian bull god Apis, he became enraged and smashed the stone tablets.

Moses's anger was righteous; the way he expressed his anger was not. We should be angry when professing Christians deny the divinity of Christ, dismiss the resurrection, and reject the infallibility of God's Word. It is fitting and right to be angry with political corruption and injustice. We should be angry with godlessness in our entertainment media and deception in our news media. We should be angry with the abortion industry, the pornography industry, and the illicit drug trade.

But our anger should be expressed in a way that produces change, justice, and redemption. We should not give in to violence or destruction as Moses did.

A Lifelong Pattern

The issue is not whether we should ever get angry but how we express our righteous anger. There are times when it would be a sin not to be angry. If we can stand by and watch people being abused and treated unjustly without our emotions being stirred, there's something morally and spiritually wrong with us.

Paul writes, "In your anger do not sin" (Eph. 4:26). How do we express righteous anger without sin? By being constructive, not destructive. By blessing instead of cursing. By focusing on the other person's feelings instead of our own. By seeking to bring joy instead of sorrow, healing instead of hurting, restoration instead of retaliation.

When Moses shouted at the people, "Listen, you rebels," he wasn't trying to help them see the error of their ways. He was simply expressing his exasperation. And when he struck the rock twice with his staff, he wasn't obeying God. He was obeying his own wrath. He was 120 years old and was still letting anger rule him as it had for most of his life. Uncontrolled anger was a lifelong pattern of behavior for Moses.

.. The people of God were camped at the edge of the promised land, having wandered in the desert for nearly forty years. The older, unbelieving generation had died off. Caleb and Joshua were the only survivors of that generation, and they were still alive because they had demonstrated faith in God.

Unfortunately, before the older generation died off, they taught their children how to gripe, murmur, complain, and feel sorry for themselves. So now a new and younger generation was complaining bitterly to Moses. In his exasperation, Moses took out his rage on the rock.

A secular psychologist would explain the story this way: Moses was simply expressing his frustration and displacing his anger onto the rock. It's not healthy to bottle up one's anger, so Moses was venting his anger with a couple of harmless whacks against an inanimate object. This was a healthy response. After all, Moses grew up in a dysfunctional family. It's only natural for him to experience explosions of anger from time to time.

God, who invented the human psyche, is not impressed by all this psychobabble. He saw something in Moses's anger that you and I might miss. Before striking the rock, Moses said, "Listen, you rebels, must we bring you water out of this rock?" Notice that word *we*. Who does Moses mean by *we*? Does he mean Moses and God? Or Moses and Aaron? That's not clear. But what is clear is that Moses has begun to take credit for the miracles of God.

Did Moses have anything to do with summoning water from rock? Did he possess magical powers? No, his job was simply to speak to the rock, and God would do the work. Did Moses perform the ten judgments against the Egyptian gods? No, God did. Did Moses provide manna from heaven to keep the Israelites alive in the desert? No, God alone did that.

But when the people complained against God, Moses took it personally. He felt like he was the victim. And when people take the victim role and pity themselves, they marinate in bitterness and resentment until they explode in rage. People who play the victim role often have problems with explosive anger.

Human Anger and God's Grace

When Moses struck the rock, God could have said to him, "You didn't do what I said. You let your anger fly out of control, so I won't turn on the water. You had your chance and you blew it."

But God didn't do that. Even though Moses disobediently struck the rock, God unleashed the fountain of blessing in the desert. Why? Because he is a God of grace. We define *grace* as God's unmerited, undeserved favor. Even though Moses disobeyed, God in his love and grace provided water for the parched throats of the Israelites and their livestock.

God graciously forgave Moses—but Moses still had to shoulder the consequences of his disobedience. He would not be allowed to enter the promised land. He stood on Mount Nebo and looked upon the promised land from a distance—but he could not possess it.

I have stood on Mount Nebo and have looked at the promised land with my own eyes. I have seen the same vista that Moses looked out on, and I get goose bumps every time I imagine the emotions Moses must have felt. He must have felt great joy to finally behold the land that was promised to Father Abraham—and great sorrow that his sin had excluded him from setting foot on that land. Our God keeps his promises and he rewards obedience.

Be angry about the things that anger God—injustice, sin, corruption, and deception. But in your anger, do not sin. When you are in a desert place, have faith and obey God. You need only to speak to the Rock of our salvation, and he will pour forth cooling streams of refreshment and blessing.

▪ QUESTIONS FOR REFLECTION AND DISCUSSION ▪

1. Moses was a great man but a flawed man. Does the example of Moses encourage and embolden your faith? Why or why not?

2. God told Moses to speak to the rock, but in his anger, Moses struck the rock with his staff. Have you ever reacted in a similar way, trying to do God's will but acting out of emotion instead of obeying God's commands? What lessons did you learn?

3. The anger of Moses was righteous; the way he expressed his anger was not. Can you recall a time when you managed your anger in a righteous way? What was the result?

4. What are some things that make you righteously angry? How have you responded?

5. Is God giving you victory over your emotions? What steps can you take to allow God to gain control of your emotions?

Trading Gold for Glory

Exodus 35:4–9; 36:6–7

During his presidency, Lyndon Baines Johnson kept a framed letter on the wall of the Oval Office. The letter was written by General Sam Houston to Reverend George W. Baines, Johnson's great-grandfather. Sam Houston was the first president of the Republic of Texas and the man for whom the city of Houston is named. President Johnson enjoyed showing the letter to White House visitors.[1] The story behind that letter is fascinating.

In his early days, Sam Houston had quite an appetite for liquor and women. He married three times. His third marriage, in 1840, was to twenty-one-year-old Margaret Lea, a devout Christian. She persuaded Houston to give up whiskey, and she begged him to receive Jesus Christ as his Lord and Savior and be baptized. Houston refused but wouldn't say why. Margaret waged a campaign to win her husband's soul

215

for the Lord. Every day, she read to him from the Bible and talked to him about God's Word. Yet he refused to commit his life to the Lord.

One day, Margaret looked out her front window and saw a family friend, Reverend George W. Baines, walking past the front gate. She ran outside, calling, "Brother Baines! I'm so glad to see you!" She invited the minister in to talk to her husband about the Lord.

Reverend Baines and Sam Houston had a long private talk. Baines learned that, early in Houston's life, his mother had taught him a distorted view of the Bible. As a result, Houston was afraid to be baptized and receive communion. Baines helped Houston understand the Bible and make up his own mind. That day, Sam Houston invited Jesus to be Lord of his life. People were amazed at the change in his life.

In gratitude to God, Houston donated to the church the equivalent of half the pastor's annual salary. Asked why he made such a large donation, Houston replied that when he was baptized, his pocketbook was baptized too.[2]

Sam Houston reminds me of the tax collector Zacchaeus, who was so overjoyed at receiving the Lord's forgiveness that he said, "Look, Lord! Here and now I give half of my possessions to the poor, and if I have cheated anybody out of anything, I will pay back four times the amount" (Luke 19:8). Sam Houston and Zacchaeus both had baptized pocketbooks.

Tithe If You Love Jesus

You have experienced the grace of God in so many ways. Have you responded to his grace? Have your pocketbook, bank account, and credit cards been baptized? Have you said, "Thank you, Lord," by your giving and spending habits?

In the 1970s, there was a bumper sticker that read, "Honk if you love Jesus." Though I appreciated Christians wanting to advertise their love for Jesus, I thought a more biblical bumper sticker would read, "Tithe if you love Jesus. Any goose can honk!"

In a 2015 report, the Giving Institute found that while charitable giving was increasing in the United States, giving to churches had dropped from 53 percent of all giving in 1987 to 32 percent. According to Nonprofits Source, an organization for nonprofit professionals, only 10–25 percent of any congregation are tithers, and 80 percent of tithers have zero credit card debt. On average, churchgoers give only 2.5 percent of their income to the church. Even more shocking, churchgoers gave 3.3 percent on average during the Great Depression, almost a full percent more than in times of prosperity. Why are Christians stingier in good economic times than during the Great Depression?

Nonprofits Source also reported that, of churchgoing families making $75,000 or more annually, only 1 percent tithed to the church. In fact, those who make less than $20,000 a year are eight times more likely to give to the church than those whose incomes exceed $75,000.[3] Clearly, the problem is not a lack of income but confused priorities—and a lack of a thankful spirit. We say we love Jesus, but we don't show it through our giving.

To many churchgoers, *giving* simply means putting money in the collection plate when the preacher guilts them into writing a check. But giving should not be prompted by guilt. It should be motivated by gratitude. As the apostle Paul writes, "Each of you should give what you have decided in your heart to give, not reluctantly or under compulsion, for God loves a cheerful giver" (2 Cor. 9:7).

That statement is much stronger in the original Greek, in which the word translated "cheerful" is the Greek word *hilaros* (from which we get the word "hilarious"). A *hilaros* giver doesn't merely smile as he puts a dollar in the plate. He is deliriously happy to give. Giving makes him kick up his heels and laugh out loud. A hilarious giver looks like Ebenezer Scrooge on Christmas morning after being visited by the three ghosts—he laughs, gives presents, and spreads joy all around.

Hilarious givers have always gladdened the heart of God. In Exodus 35, we see Moses announcing God's command for the building of the tabernacle, Israel's first house of worship:

> Moses said to the whole Israelite community, "This is what the LORD has commanded: From what you have, take an offering for the LORD. Everyone who is willing is to bring to the LORD an offering of gold, silver and bronze; blue, purple and scarlet yarn and fine linen; goat hair; ram skins dyed red and another type of durable leather; acacia wood; olive oil for the light; spices for the anointing oil and for the fragrant incense; and onyx stones and other gems to be mounted on the ephod and breastpiece." (vv. 4–9)

Note that phrase: "Everyone who is willing." There was no arm-twisting, no guilting. In Exodus 36, we read the result of those offerings: "Then Moses gave an order and they sent this word throughout the camp: 'No man or woman is to make anything else as an offering for the sanctuary.' And so the people were restrained from bringing more, because what they already had was more than enough to do all the work" (vv. 6–7).

Moses makes it clear that God is more concerned with a believer's heart than his money. God wants his people to give out of gratitude. He is looking for a willing heart, a joyful heart, a generous heart. Jesus affirmed this motive when he said, "For where your treasure is, there your heart will be also" (Matt. 6:21).

There's no greater way to express gratitude to God than through giving. Does it melt our hearts to remember the agony Jesus endured on the cross for us? If so, it won't be a burden to give to God. It will be a privilege.

Are you truly committed to Christ? Then demonstrate your commitment through your giving. You might say, "There are other ways I show my commitment." But Jesus didn't say, "Where your singing is, there your heart will be also." He didn't say, "Where your church attendance is, there your heart will be also." He didn't say, "Where your witnessing is, there your heart will be also." Singing praise songs, attending church, and witnessing are great signs of commitment, but nothing outshines our generous giving to God.

When I was ordained to the ministry, I didn't think I needed to be a faithful giver. I had my rationalizations all worked out as to why God didn't expect me to tithe: "Lord, I gave you myself. I'm in full-time ministry. You know how little money I make. You can't expect me to give as much as a Christian with a well-paying job."

After I had been in ministry a few years, God brought me under conviction. I felt him saying, "Youssef, hand over the cash!" I had been deceiving myself. Since I came clean with God over giving, he has showered me with countless blessings. If you are not joyfully giving to God, you are impoverishing yourself and missing out on God's best.

God Tabernacles with His People

God told Moses to build a tabernacle, a huge tent, as a place for God to dwell among his people. The tabernacle was a stadium-sized tent at the top of a hill. Every Israelite could step outside the family tent and look toward the hilltop and see the tabernacle of the Lord.

The tabernacle foreshadowed the coming of Emmanuel ("God with us"), the Lord Jesus Christ. As John wrote in his Gospel, "The Word became flesh and made his dwelling among us" (John 1:14). In the original language, the phrase "made his dwelling" is one word that means "tabernacled." John tells us that, in Jesus, God became flesh and tabernacled among us.

The psalmist writes:

> Yet you are enthroned as the Holy One;
>   you are the one Israel praises. (Ps. 22:3)

I think the King James Version comes closer to the original meaning: "But thou art holy, O thou that inhabitest the praises of Israel." That's a powerful statement: God inhabits the praises of his people.

Many Christians think that "praises" means songs of praise. But praise means so much more than merely singing songs. Praising God includes sacrifice. It means we give something to God—something we value dearly. That's why the Bible tells us, "Through Jesus, therefore, let us continually offer to God a sacrifice of praise—the fruit of lips that openly profess his name" (Heb. 13:15).

We offer God a sacrifice of praise when we give God an offering that costs us in a material way. If we praise him with our lips but we sacrifice nothing, then our so-called praise is just empty words. Empty praise does not bless the Lord, nor will it be blessed by the Lord.

In their journey from slavery to nationhood, the Israelites saw God provide for their needs. They saw the grace of God, the provision of God, and the power of God. He provided an escape from slavery to freedom. He parted the Red Sea—then closed the sea and drowned their enemies. He provided sweet water from bitter water. He provided a cloud by day and a pillar of fire at night. He provided all this and more.

By his power, God could have provided the tabernacle as a miracle from heaven. But God wanted the people to build the tabernacle and donate the materials themselves. Why?

Imagine a father who gives his son everything. The son takes and takes and gives nothing back. He grows to manhood without ever lifting a finger. He feels entitled to receive and never give anything in return. I ask you: What sort of husband will he grow up to be? What sort of citizen will he be? What sort of church member will he be? Will he be emotionally and spiritually healthy—or will he be arrogant and self-centered?

God wanted Israel to be emotionally and spiritually healthy. He was raising the Israelites to be mature and giving, like their heavenly Father. In the same way, God wants us as Christians to be emotionally and spiritually healthy, to be mature and giving, to be like Christ. How does God accomplish this in our lives? One way is by teaching us to give sacrificially.

God has blessed us in so many ways by his grace. So what is a healthy, mature response to all we have received? Gratitude. Giving. The sacrifice of praise. Yet many of us only give a few crumbs back to God.

The Firstfruit

God commanded the Israelites to give the first 10 percent to the Levites for the support of the priesthood. The Levites were in full-time ministry and had no businesses, so it was incumbent on the Israelites to support the priests. Households were to give a second 10 percent as the firstfruit—a tithe set aside out of the family income before any other money was spent—for the support and maintenance of the tabernacle. The Israelites were also required to set aside a third 10 percent every third year to meet the needs of the poor.

On top of these three required offerings, the people would make a freewill offering of any amount. Why did God place such a high demand on his people? Did he want to impoverish them? No. What God wanted was for them to understand that the secret of blessing is giving. God is the great Giver, and we are to pattern our giving after his.

God teaches us how to give through Israel's pattern of giving. When we give the firstfruit to God, we are saying, "Lord, I trust you to provide for my tomorrow. Lord, I trust you to meet all my future needs. Lord, I trust you to provide for whatever I might face in the future."

Why do we call these offerings the "firstfruit"? In Bible times, people lived in a farm-based society. At harvesttime, farmers received the reward—the fruit—of their labor. God told his people to bring the first tenth of the yield—the firstfruit—to the priests as a sign of obedience. All harvesting stopped until the firstfruit was presented—then the harvest could continue.

The Israelites called the firstfruit *bikkurim*, meaning "a promise to come." The Israelites viewed the firstfruit as a sign of trust in God's promise of provision, an investment in his future blessing. This offering is called the firstfruit because it is from the top, not the bottom. It is the best, not the least.

Israel later adopted an attitude of giving God the leftovers instead of the firstfruit—and this attitude brought judgment upon the nation. God, speaking through the prophet Malachi, said:

"Will a mere mortal rob God? Yet you rob me.

"But you ask, 'How are we robbing you?'

"In tithes and offerings. You are under a curse—your whole nation—because you are robbing me. Bring the whole tithe into the storehouse, that there may be food in my house. Test me in this," says the LORD Almighty, "and see if I will not throw open the floodgates of heaven and pour out so much blessing that there will not be room enough to store it. I will prevent pests from devouring your crops, and the vines in your fields will not drop their fruit before it is ripe," says the LORD Almighty. "Then all the nations will call you blessed, for yours will be a delightful land," says the LORD Almighty. (Mal. 3:8–12)

The God who spoke these words to Israel is the God who created our universe, which is ninety-three billion light-years in diameter, containing hundreds of billions of galaxies, with each galaxy containing one hundred billion more stars. This same God could have spoken a single word, and a glorious tabernacle would have miraculously appeared on the hilltop. But God chose to build the tabernacle through the sacrifices of his people.

When God calls us to give, it's not because he's poor and must beg for donations. It's because we need to give. Giving brings blessings into our lives.

"Stop Giving!"

Notice the spirit of extravagant generosity in Exodus 35–36. The people are so grateful for God's blessings that they give and give until Moses says, "Stop giving! You've been so generous, we have more than we can use!" Imagine a preacher standing up and saying to the congregation, "Ushers, don't pass the offering plate! Congregation, stop giving! We have more than enough for the ministry of the church and missions and helping the poor!"

Moses told the people, "No man or woman is to make anything else as an offering for the sanctuary." Why? Because the priests had already collected more than enough. Everyone freely gave from a grateful heart, and the donations exceeded the need.

While tithing was the first tangible test of Israel's *obedience* to God, the freewill offering was the first real test of Israel's *love* for God. The people gave out of grateful, loving hearts as an act of worship. That spirit of giving was so contagious that everyone gave more than enough.

If you truly have nothing to give, you owe no tithe. A tenth of nothing is nothing. But if you say, "I have nothing and can't afford to give to God—in fact, I am deep in debt and can barely afford my credit card bills each month," then perhaps you should have a talk with a Christian debt counselor.

It's one thing if you have a lot of debt because you have hospital bills or your business failed. It's quite another thing if you're paying off countless restaurant meals and Starbucks lattes, a sailboat and jet skis, and vacations in Maui. If you aren't tithing because your credit cards are maxed out, you're not giving God the firstfruit. Your priorities are upside-down.

When the people of Israel were swept off their feet by a spirit of giving, they were transformed from a mob of gripers and complainers into a congregation of joyful worshipers. There are few more joyful experiences than getting swept up in a spirit of giving.

A similar event occurred four centuries later. King David challenged Israel to give a freewill offering above and beyond the tithe to build the temple. David prayed:

> But who am I, and who are my people, that we should be able to give as generously as this? Everything comes from you, and we have given you only what comes from your hand. We are foreigners and strangers in your sight, as were all our ancestors. Our days on earth are like a shadow, without hope. LORD our God, all this abundance that we have provided for building you a temple for your Holy Name comes from your hand, and all of it belongs to you. I know, my God, that you test the heart and are pleased with integrity. All these things I have given willingly and with honest intent. And now I have seen with joy how willingly your people who are here have

given to you. LORD, the God of our fathers Abraham, Isaac and Israel, keep these desires and thoughts in the hearts of your people forever, and keep their hearts loyal to you. (1 Chron. 29:14–18)

David measured the people's loyalty to God by their willingness to exchange their gold for God's glory.

Love Is Freedom

There is a virulent false teaching that has infected many churches, impoverished countless families, ruined countless lives, and shaken the faith of countless believers. This false teaching is called the prosperity gospel. It teaches that God wants his people to be wealthy, healthy, and successful, and if we have enough faith, God will give us material blessings. According to this false gospel, sickness and poverty are curses to be broken by increasing our faith—and by donating to prosperity gospel preachers.

You will never hear me say that if you tithe, you will get a Rolls-Royce from God. If you gratefully, cheerfully give to God, he will bless you—but that blessing may have nothing to do with keeping you healthy or making you wealthy.

Let me suggest an analogy of how our giving should flow from our love for God. Imagine a father telling his son, "I'd like you to take the daughter of a business associate on a date tomorrow night."

The young man groans. "I had other plans. She and I probably have nothing in common."

"You'd really be helping me out, son."

226

"Oh, all right."

This young man obeyed because his father asked him, and he loves his father.

The next night, the boy meets the young lady, they go out—and he finds her fascinating. She's the girl of his dreams. Before long, they are boyfriend and girlfriend.

Why is this young man still taking the girl out on dates? Is it because he still feels obligated to his father? No, he has a new motivation. He's in love with the girl and wants to be with her. Giving to God is a lot like that.

In the beginning, you give the firstfruit because God commands it and you want to obey. But soon you experience the joy of giving cheerfully of your own free will. The more you give, the greater your joy.

It's not wrong to give out of obligation and obedience. That's how you first learn to give. But once you experience that joy, you want to give out of gratitude and love. You are free to give joyfully, extravagantly, hilariously. Love is the freedom to give joyfully.

In our church, we do not ask for donations every week. We don't put a thermometer on the wall and show you when we are up and when we are down. We do take pledge cards, but we ask our churchgoers not to sign the cards. We don't want to know who has pledged what, and we don't want anyone to feel pressured.

Also, we tell non-Christians, "Please don't give to the church. God wants you to give him your heart before you give him a single cent." God has provided all the resources we have ever needed to fund the work of The Church of The Apostles. God has provided all we need through the faithfulness of his people, without pressure or guilt.

I hope that you will trade your gold for God's glory. Don't miss out on the blessing that can come only from giving generously. Don't nickel-and-dime God. Don't give grudgingly. Don't give with selfish motives, expecting a quid pro quo from God.

Shout for joy as you offer God your gold—then prepare to be amazed when you experience his glory.

■ QUESTIONS FOR REFLECTION AND DISCUSSION ■

1. What is your primary motivation for giving to God? Do you think it's a godly motivation? Why or why not?

2. Have you seen God provide for you in amazing ways? How does counting your blessings affect your desire to give to God?

3. What is the firstfruit in your life? Do you give the firstfruit to God? Why or why not?

4. Are there changes you need to make in your spending, your use of credit and debt, and your lifestyle to become a hilarious giver? What goals do you want to set to become a hilarious giver?

Notes

Introduction

1. John MacArthur, *Hebrews*, MacArthur New Testament Commentary (Chicago: Moody, 1983), 350–51.

2. Arthur Tappan Pierson, ed., *The Missionary Review of the World*, vol. 22, *January to December 1899* (New York: Funk & Wagnalls, 1899), 357.

Chapter 1 Complete Surrender

1. Pat Williams, *Character Carved in Stone: The 12 Core Virtues of West Point That Build Leaders and Produce Success* (Grand Rapids: Revell, 2019), 124.

2. D. P. Thomson, "Quotes by and about Eric Liddell from D P Thomson's 'Scotland's Greatest Athlete,'" Eric Liddell Centre, accessed February 24, 2020, https://www.ericliddell.org/about-us/eric-liddell/quotations/.

3. Eric T. Eichinger with Eva Marie Everson, *The Final Race: The Incredible World War II Story of the Olympian Who Inspired* Chariots of Fire (Carol Stream, IL: Tyndale, 2018), 62–63.

4. Sally Magnusson, *The Flying Scotsman: A Biography* (Stroud, Gloucestershire, UK: History Press, 2009), 167.

Chapter 3 Stepping-Stones to Leadership

1. First Five Years Fund, "Why It Matters: Brain Development," Ffyf.org, accessed February 3, 2020, https://www.ffyf.org/why-it-matters/brain-development/.

2. George H. C. Macgregor, "Personal Consecration," in *Northfield Echoes: Northfield Conference Addresses for 1897*, ed. Delavan L. Pierson, vol. 4 (East Northfield, MA: Northfield Echoes, 1897), 478–79.

Chapter 4 Hitting Bottom

1. J. E. Kaufmann and H. W. Kaufmann, *The American GI in Europe in World War II: D-Day: Storming Ashore* (Mechanicsburg, PA: Stackpole, 2009), 147.
2. Exodus also calls Jethro by the name Reuel.
3. Tommy Hilliker, "God's Promise of the Holy Spirit," July 7, 2019, Saddleback Church, podcast audio transcribed by the author.

Chapter 5 Confronting the Lie

1. Amy B. Wang, "'Post-Truth' Named 2016 Word of the Year by Oxford Dictionaries," *Washington Post*, November 16, 2016, https://www.washington post.com/news/the-fix/wp/2016/11/16/post-truth-named-2016-word-of-the-year -by-oxford-dictionaries/.
2. David Limbaugh, *Persecution: How Liberals Are Waging War against Christians* (Washington, DC: Regnery, 2003), 140–41.
3. Jay Dennis, *The Jesus Habits: Exercising the Spiritual Disciplines of Jesus* (Nashville: Broadman & Holman, 2005), 51.
4. Sadhu Sundar Singh, "I Have Decided to Follow Jesus," public domain.
5. Anthony Zinni, Ronald Keys, and Frank Bowman, "US Military Refuses to Be 'Too Late' on Climate Change," *The (Tacoma) News Tribune*, October 28, 2014, https://www.thenewstribune.com/opinion/article25890007.html.
6. Bill Ridgers, ed., *Book of Business Quotations* (Hoboken, NJ: Wiley, 2012), 175.
7. Erasmus, "Why Koran Readings in Anglican Churches Preoccupy the Mighty," *The Economist*, January 27, 2017, https://www.economist.com/erasmus /2017/01/27/why-koran-readings-in-anglican-churches-preoccupy-the-mighty.
8. Lita Cosner and Scott Gillis, "Pastor Andy Stanley Says the Bible Is Too Hard to Defend," Creation.com, September 22, 2016, https://creation.com/andy -stanley-rebuttal.

Chapter 7 The Firstborn and the Lamb

1. Richard Dawkins, *Outgrowing God: A Beginner's Guide* (New York: Random House, 2019), 52.
2. Jerry Pierce, "The Cross of Christ Divides Humanity," *Decision* magazine, February 25, 2016, https://billygraham.org/decision-magazine/march-2016/the -cross-of-christ-divides-humanity/.

Chapter 8 Faith—or Fear?

1. "Spanish Armada Defeated (July 29, 1588)," History, last updated July 25, 2019, https://www.history.com/this-day-in-history/spanish-armada-defeated.
2. Dr. E. Stanley Jones, quoted in Dr. Grant Martin, *Transformed by Thorns* (Wheaton: Victor Books, 1985), 95.
3. Barna Group, "What Faith Looks Like in the Workplace," Barna, October 30, 2018, https://www.barna.com/research/faith-workplace/.

Chapter 9 Wandering from the Truth

1. James E. Adams, *A Treasury of Living Faith: Catholic Devotions for Every Day of the Year* (Fenton, MO: Creative Communications for the Parish, 1991), 3.
2. Herbert Lockyer, *All about the Holy Spirit: A Full Inquiry into the Attributes of the Holy Spirit* (Peabody, MA: Hendrickson, 2011), 42.

Chapter 10 The Danger of Discontentment

1. Bob Perks, "I Wish You Enough," StoriesForPreaching.com, accessed September 20, 2019, https://storiesforpreaching.com/category/sermonillustrations /contentment/.
2. Steve Taylor, PhD, "Happiness Comes from Giving, Not Buying and Having," *PsychologyToday*, January 9, 2015, https://www.psychologytoday.com /intl/blog/out-the-darkness/201501/happiness-comes-giving-not-buying-and -having?amp.

Chapter 11 Victory through Surrender

1. Dennis Prager, "Compassion and the Decline of America," Townhall, March 20, 2007, https://townhall.com/columnists/dennisprager/2007/03/20/compassion -and-the-decline-of-america-n747220.
2. Pat Williams, *Ahead of the Game: The Pat Williams Story* (Grand Rapids: Revell, 2014), 175.
3. Mary Hollingsworth, *Fireside Stories: Heartwarming Tales of Life, Love, and Laughter* (Nashville: Word, 2000), 123.
4. "Marathon Man Akhwari Demonstrates Superhuman Spirit," Olympic.org, accessed February 20, 2020, https://www.olympic.org/news/marathon-man-akh wari-demonstrates-superhuman-spirit.

Chapter 12 Tempted to Compromise

1. Steve Tignor, "1989: Image Is Everything—Andre Agassi's Infamous Ad," Tennis.com, August 30, 2015, http://www.tennis.com/pro-game/2015/08/image -everything-andre-agassis-infamous-ad/55425/.
2. Quoted in Robby Gallaty, *Growing Up: How to Be a Disciple Who Makes Disciples* (Bloomington, IN: CrossBooks, 2013), 134.
3. Margaret Thatcher, "Interview for Press Association (10th Anniversary as Prime Minister)," May 3, 1989, Margaret Thatcher Foundation, https://www.mar garetthatcher.org/document/107427.

Chapter 13 The Envy of Critics

1. "5 People Who Threw Shade on George Washington," New England Historical Society, accessed February 20, 2020, http://www.newenglandhistorical society.com/5-people-threw-shade-george-washington/.

2. "Evidence for the Unpopular Mr. Lincoln," American Battlefield Trust, accessed February 20, 2020, https://www.battlefields.org/learn/articles/evidence -unpopular-mr-lincoln.

3. Mike Bundrant, "The Abe Lincoln Method of Handling Criticism," INLP Center, accessed February 20, 2020, https://inlpcenter.org/abraham-lincoln-hand ling-criticism/.

Chapter 14 Lord of the Impossible

1. Richard Watson, "Timeline of Failed Predictions (Part 1)," *Fast Company*, December 1, 2010, https://www.fastcompany.com/1706712/timeline-failed-pre dictions-part-1.

Chapter 15 Wrongful Wrath

1. Frederick Buechner, *Beyond Words: Daily Readings in the ABC's of Faith* (San Francisco: HarperSanFrancisco, 2004), 18.

Chapter 16 Trading Gold for Glory

1. Nick Kotz, *Judgment Days: Lyndon Baines Johnson, Martin Luther King, Jr., and the Laws That Changed America* (Boston: Houghton Mifflin, 2005), 244.

2. James L. Haley, *Sam Houston* (Norman, OK: University of Oklahoma Press, 2002), xii–xiii, 329, 331.

3. Jayson D. Bradley, "Church Giving Statistics, 2019 Edition," Pushpay, July 18, 2018, https://pushpay.com/blog/church-giving-statistics/.

Michael Youssef is the founder and president of Leading The Way with Dr. Michael Youssef (www.LTW.org), a worldwide ministry that leads the way for people living in spiritual darkness to discover the light of Christ through the creative use of media and on-the-ground ministry teams. He is also the founding pastor of The Church of The Apostles in Atlanta, Georgia. The author of *Life-Changing Prayers* and *Counting Stars in an Empty Sky*, Youssef lives with his wife in Atlanta. They have four grown children and ten grandchildren.

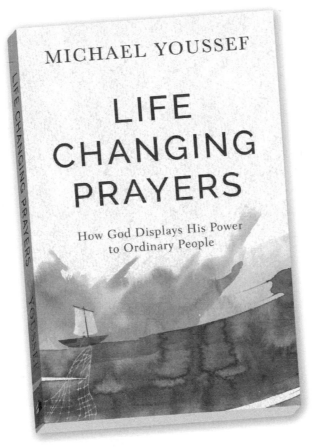

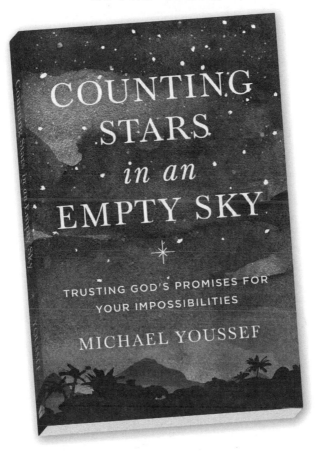

Connect with
Dr. Michael Youssef!

MichaelYoussef.com

Connect with

BakerBooks

Relevant. Intelligent. Engaging.

Sign up for announcements about new and upcoming titles at

BakerBooks.com/SignUp

@ReadBakerBooks